Making Lemonade

Parents Transforming Special Needs

CANDEE FICK

This book is dedicated to
my precious daughter, Anna.
Without you, I wouldn't be the woman I am today.
I love you, Princess.

CONTENTS

ACKNOWLEDGMENTS

This book that you hold in your hands has been a labor of love over the past four years. My own journey as the parent of a special needs child has found wisdom, encouragement and support through a large group of people including the CdLS Foundation, the CdLS Online support group, therapists, doctors, teachers and paraprofessionals. Without them, I'd have lost my sanity a long time ago. Thank you.

I also need to thank Jan, Linda, Lisa, Lori, Sherilyn, Shannon and Roxanne for sharing their stories and waiting patiently as I struggled to get these words into print. Ladies, you are a true inspiration!

Next up are my husband, kids, parents and extended family. Thanks for your patience as I brainstormed out loud and spent countless hours in front of my computer.

Last, but certainly not least, I thank my Heavenly Father for His gifts. For Anna and what she has taught me about unconditional love. For writing and the means to encourage others on this journey called life. To Him be the glory.

1 - IN THE KITCHEN

Being a parent is hard work.

It starts for mothers with nausea followed by back aches, swollen feet, stretch marks, heartburn and frequent nocturnal trips to the bathroom leading up to labor and delivery. And that is only the beginning of the journey.

Sleep deprivation, around-the-clock feedings and stacks of diapers give way to baby-proofing the house, Dora the Explorer and potty training. Learning to ride a bike, first days of school, making friends, sports and homework, music lessons, learning to drive, first dates . . . and the journey of parenthood continues. As parents, we teach manners and morals, faith and friendship and everything else we think our children need in order to grow up to honor God and be productive adults in society.

Being a parent is difficult enough when things are typical. But what if life brings a few sour experiences along the way? These issues can range from bed-wetting to bullies, rejection to rebellion, accidents to allergies and cleaning rooms to the common cold. Some parents deal with additional truckloads of issues in the form of:

> - Learning disabilities including dyslexia, dyscalculia and dysgraphia – an estimated one in seven individuals[i]

- Asthma – the most common chronic disease of childhood affecting as many as one in 20 children[ii]
- AD/HD – an estimated three to five percent of children or at least one in a class of 25 to 30[iii]
- Autism spectrum disorders – an estimated one in 110 children and almost one in 94 boys[iv]
- Cystic Fibrosis – an estimated one in 31 are carriers of the defective gene[v]
- Down syndrome – an estimated one in 700 live births[vi]
- Cerebral palsy – an estimated 8000 babies are diagnosed each year[vii]
- Legg-Calve-Perthes Disease – an estimated one in 1200 children[viii]
- Spina Bifida – an estimated seven in 10,000 live births[ix]
- Tuberous sclerosis – an estimated one in 6000 live births[x]
- Cornelia de Lange syndrome – an estimated one in 10,000[xi]
- Acute lymphoblastic leukemia (ALL) – the most common malignancy diagnosed in children, representing nearly one third of all pediatric cancers with an annual incidence of 30.9 cases per million people.[xii]

The list of additional issues facing parents goes on and on. Sour parenting experiences are as common as they are varied.

Personally, my daughter was born with Cornelia de Lange syndrome resulting in developmental and speech delays, mental retardation, autistic-like behaviors, growth delays, dislocated elbows, acid reflux and more. My youngest son was on a respirator at birth. He then developed asthma triggered by allergies to cats, dogs, horses and locust trees and therefore had trouble breathing whenever he visited his grandparent's house. A neighborhood bully with a golf club sent my daughter to the emergency room for staples in her scalp. My oldest son went missing for several hours one afternoon. One of my nephews has

Legg-Perthes disease where his hipbone died, dissolved, and had to re-grow.

How can a parent handle the sour experiences that come along as a part of life? That is the question to be answered within the pages of this book. If we consider these sour experiences to be like lemons, a sour fruit, then how we approach, process and transform those lemons could be compared to the process of making lemonade.

For the purpose of this book, let's make something clear. A lemon is absolutely **not** a mutated, defective, rotten or unripe piece of fruit. The lemons we will discuss do not bear the negative connotation of a wrongfully advertised car or a cosmic trick played on the unsuspecting.

One struggle parents already face is seeing our children as God sees them and not as the world labels them – "defective." God designed our children in the womb and He saw that all of creation was good. Our children are fearfully and wonderfully made.[xiii] God used just as much care and thoughtfulness when He chose my child's special gifts as He did with every other person on this planet. Anna isn't mentally handicapped because God forgot her or ran out of material. Whatever the causes of her mental disability, God gifted her for His own unique purposes. As one saying goes, "God doesn't make junk."

So, a lemon is simply a sour experience. While the sour experiences (or lemons) may be associated with a child, the child is not the lemon. Rather, the issues related to our children are the lemons.

When it comes to lemons as fruit, in small doses they add a unique flavor and zest to food ranging from lemon chicken to lemon meringue pie. Nothing is more satisfying on a hot summer day than a tall glass of ice-cold lemonade. Lemon juice is also used in cleaners to cut through grime and leave a fresh scent. The lemons in life also add a flavor of their own and cut to our heart, cleaning out the clutter of misplaced priorities.

Every parent faces at least one type of lemon along the way. Whether they are short-term or long-term issues, we can approach and process these lemons in a way similar to making lemonade. All recipes for lemonade (and I've included several in appendix just for fun) contain the same basic ingredients: lemon juice, sugar and water. Like lemonade's mixture of sugar and lemons, the sweet and sour of having children gets mixed together until they become inseparable. It's impossible to have one without the other.

Recipes for lemonade also contain the same steps. Mirroring these steps, we will explore the initial pucker reaction and the juicing process where it can feel as though one's guts are being ripped out. The next ingredient, sugar, is compared to hope and faith in the knowledge that God is in control and that we can do all things through His strength. Other fruit or siblings can be added to the mix and add a unique flavor combination of their own. Watered down by the normal parts of life, the ingredients are stirred by parents putting action to their faith within the pitcher of support from family and friends. After a period of waiting or chilling, we are able to sit back and enjoy the end result as well as share it with a friend.

The practical strategies shared within the pages of this book have been gleaned from the experiences of parents facing multiple lemons or a lifetime supply. These parents are busy making lemonade in their own kitchens of life. In addition to sharing my experiences, you will also meet:

- Sherilyn, whose oldest son was born with mild cerebral palsy and then years later faced three and a half years of chemotherapy when her youngest son was diagnosed with acute lymphoblastic leukemia.
- Roxanne, who lost a child to SIDS (Sudden

Infant Death Syndrome) and then had a son born with mosaic Down syndrome.

- Lisa, who has two sons within the autism spectrum of disorders including one with Asberger's syndrome.
- Lori, who has a son with autism as well as another son with ADD.
- Jan, who has a daughter with tuberous sclerosis resulting in mental retardation, autism, seizures, ADHD and a rare inoperable brain tumor.
- Shannon, who has a son with autism who was also born with a cleft palette.
- Linda, whose firstborn son was diagnosed with an extremely rare, and usually fatal, form of cancer.

Why am I writing this book? Because I'm in the kitchen making lemonade every day. Some days my batch of lemonade is really sour. Other days it is sweeter or more watered down. Tomorrow, there will be new lemons and the process repeated.

As we start this journey, please don't compare your lemons to someone else's. You will either feel envy that "They have it so easy" or guilt because "My child isn't as bad off as their child." A parent dealing with mental retardation or behavior issues can't imagine transferring a child in and out of a wheelchair or flushing a feeding tube. And vice versa.

No matter the issue, the basic emotions are the same for all of us. Simply because we didn't get what we expected as parents.

Because the recipe for lemonade contains the same ingredients and steps, it can be used whether you are making one glass, one pitcher or enough to serve an army. Each of us has our own batch of lemons – whether the supply fills a bowl, a shopping cart or an orchard – and we have the opportunity to transform them into something to enjoy and share. In the end, we may find that the process has transformed us.

As we journey together and learn how to make lemonade from life's lemons, feel free to laugh and to cry. Be encouraged that you are not alone in the struggles of being a parent. There is hope for a wonderful end product. In fact, take a little time at the end of each chapter to get to work in your kitchen.

Let's make some lemonade!

In Your Kitchen

1. Make a list of the lemons you have encountered so far as a parent.

2. Put a star next to those you are currently facing. These are the ones we will focus on throughout the pages of this book.

2 - TASTING LEMONS

Gene felt a little self-conscious as he approached the doctor. His wife had urged him to find out if there was a problem with their newborn son because she hadn't seen him yet that morning. "Yes, we think maybe your baby is a mongoloid," the doctor replied. Gene was stunned, and then got so mad at the coldhearted delivery of the news that he drew back to knock the doctor through the glass partition by the nurse's station. Instead, he passed out before his fist could hit anything but the floor. The news that his son had what is now known as Down syndrome was the furthest thing from his mind.[xiv]

What happens when you taste something extremely sour? Does your mouth immediately feel as though your cheeks are greeting over your tongue? Do you try to spit it out? Do your eyes water? Does your entire face contort? Do you say "Yuck?"

Our reactions vary and sometimes depend on our previous experiences. Having just eaten a piece of cake or ice cream, the sour taste seems much worse. On the other hand, if our mouth was already accustomed to neutral or sour flavors, the reaction to another sour food might be minimal. There is no right or wrong way to react when tasting a lemon.

How would I have reacted in Gene's place when he received that stunning news? I honestly don't know. None of us knows how we will react in the face of bad news until it happens. And then our reactions are as varied as our emotions – anger, violence, grief, disbelief, shock, or tears. Like tasting lemons, there is no right or wrong way to feel. Our immediate reaction and feelings are what they are. The extent of our pucker also depends on what has come before the news.

Journey with these parents as they taste their lemons. Notice whether the events leading up to a diagnosis helped reduce their initial reaction or not.

Shannon knew something was wrong with Noah within 24 hours of his birth. She was trying to breastfeed her newborn but he couldn't latch on. She even tried to give him a bottle but he couldn't latch on and suck.

"Something is wrong. My child won't feed," Shannon told the nurses.

"He's new. You're a new mom. He has to get used to you and you to him," they replied. "Keep trying and he'll get it."

"But, I've been through this before with my first son. There's more to this than him just needing to figure out how to nurse." Shannon knew something was wrong because Noah couldn't suck.

When their pediatrician arrived the next morning, he discovered that Noah had a cleft palette. While Shannon and her husband Ray were relieved to learn why Noah was having difficulty feeding, they were also saddened. Shannon knew there were surgeries ahead and Noah would experience pain as a result.

Within three weeks, they were referred to a cleft clinic only to receive more bad news. At the clinic, Noah was also diagnosed with low muscle tone and Pierre Robin syndrome. The characteristics of Pierre Robin are a cleft palette, receding chin, hearing loss and some learning disabilities.

At two years of age, things changed again. Specialists diagnosed Noah as having dyspraxia dysarthria. Dyspraxia related to the speech coordination of getting what Noah wanted to say from his brain to his mouth. Dysarthria involved the low muscle tone, where even if Noah could get what he wanted to say to his mouth, his articulating muscles would not work. At that point, the specialists felt that the Pierre Robin syndrome label no longer applied and Noah was diagnosed with an "undiagnosed syndrome." How's that for helpful?

The journey wasn't over yet. Shannon and Ray still didn't know what they were dealing with but knew there were other issues. Every year it was something new. After seeing other children at various therapy groups, they began to believe Noah had a high functioning form of autism based on his characteristics and quirks.

Noah was officially diagnosed with autism at age 4. Shannon said, "At that point, some people are really sad and go through a grieving period. But with us, it was more of a sense of relief that we finally had a diagnosis and we knew what we were dealing with."

Being a perfectionist and over-achiever, it was no surprise that my first pregnancy was by the book. Every doctor's appointment showed the exact amount of expected growth and my obstetrician would tease me about being perfect. That is until gestational week 34.

I was scheduled to meet the other partner in the practice. The ritual measurement of growth was repeated twice and my chart was consulted. "Mrs. Fick, I'm getting the same measurement as your last appointment two weeks ago. It might be because a different person is taking the measurement but I would like you to return in a week just to be sure."

Puzzled but comforted by the explanation, I didn't think much of it. At my appointment the next week, my regular obstetrician measured my large abdomen and then measured again. With a furrowed brow, he rang for the nurse to prepare the ultrasound machine. "I'm getting the same measurement as your 32-week appointment and I'd like to take a look."

The ultrasound revealed that part of the placenta was aging prematurely and therefore the baby wasn't getting as much support as before. The next day, my husband and I traveled to a different hospital for a more detailed ultrasound. This time we finally learned that we were having a girl and that one of the vessels in her umbilical cord was flowing both ways. In lay terms, that meant that our daughter was working overtime to pump blood and didn't have energy left to grow.

We named her Anna Joy and notified family and friends so they could pray. Anna was monitored every couple of days in the doctor's office until we reached 37 and a half weeks. At that point, the plan was to have an amniocentesis procedure to confirm lung maturity and then get her out where she could grow. While hooked up to a monitor before the procedure, I had random contractions. During one contraction, bells and whistles went off and nurses flooded in to poke at my belly since Anna's heart rate had dropped dangerously low. She recovered quickly and we breathed a sigh of relief.

Once the results of the amniocentesis were back, I was induced for delivery. About an hour into regular contractions, the bells and whistles went off again. Anna didn't like labor any more than I did and she was delivered via c-section weighing just 4 pounds and 5 ounces.

With the history of the previous weeks, I was prepared to hear about problems. Instead, aside from getting worn out from nursing and needing to be bottle-fed for the first few weeks, Anna was declared healthy and we were sent home. Her growth rate took off until about 6 months of age when it slowed down. Our pediatrician assured us that all children level off at that age and find their own growth curve to follow. At 9 months, we began to worry again about her growth and, at our pediatrician's advice, began adding butter and powdered milk to her food to increase the calories. Anna's developmental milestones, like pulling up to stand, were behind but we attributed the delays to her small size. You can't pull yourself up if you can't reach the table, right?

At 12 months, Anna weighed just 13 pounds. I worried about how tiny she was but everywhere I turned people told me about some other child who was 13 pounds at a year and "Look at them now." I wanted to be reassured by their comments but in my gut, I knew something was wrong and felt like I must be a poor mother. Pregnant with our second child, I worried and then worried some more. Our pediatrician was also concerned about her growth and we discussed testing at Children's Hospital after the new baby was born and things settled down.

When Anna was 16 months old and I had a newborn baby at home, I received a call from our pediatrician. "Mrs. Fick, I don't want to alarm you but I need to let you know that our office received an anonymous phone call today threatening to turn your family in to Social Services for not feeding your daughter. If that happened, I would also be contacted and, because we are very aware of her growth issues and are working on them, it would be easily resolved. However, I'm sending in the referral to Children's Hospital immediately."

So, within a few weeks, I was at Children's Hospital with my mother to help carry my two children. The first doctor we saw looked at us with critical eyes and didn't seem to believe me when I told her how much Anna ate. The doctor ordered several tests including growth hormones and a chromosome screen and sent us home with a dietary diary to fill out. At our next appointment, the doctor's tune had changed to puzzlement. "Her test results came back all normal and she is getting more than enough calories daily to catch up growth. I think the problem may be an absorption issue in her intestines. I want to refer you to another specialist but our protocol is that you need to be seen by the genetics department first."

I scheduled an appointment with genetics but it was several months before we could be seen. As I filled out a family history and sent in pictures prior to our appointment, I was irritated that we had to wait so long. I just wanted to get the genetics appointment behind us so we could move on to the real answers and help Anna grow. Her development was falling further behind but growth was our main concern. In fact, I was so sure genetics was not the reason, my husband went to work that day while my mother came along to help with my two non-walking children.

On September 28, 1998, our lives changed. Anna was 22 months old and spent the appointment cruising around the furniture in the examination room. After getting an initial history and examining Anna, the geneticist and a tag-a-long graduate student went out in the hall to confer. They returned carrying a medical textbook and several pieces of paper.

"We believe that Anna has a rare genetic condition called Cornelia de Lange syndrome. As you can see from these pictures, affected individuals resemble each other." I looked at the textbook page and felt like I was looking at pictures of Anna. "The syndrome affects growth and development. Anna will probably walk and probably talk but we recommend you get some therapy right away for her development." As we left, the graduate student handed me several pages of information printed off the Internet.

My mom and I somehow got the kids back to the car and buckled into their car seats. I remember sitting there thinking "It's not my fault that she is so small." This syndrome is characterized by slow growth and even explained her growth issues before she was born. The immediate feeling of relief was like a weight had been lifted off of my chest and I could breathe again.

Then I began to read the pages in my hand and saw words like "mental retardation" and "developmental delay." I read the pages from the Cornelia de Lange Syndrome Foundation aloud and my mom and I dissected and memorized every nugget all the way home. It was starting to sink in that my beautiful little girl might not be able to get A's in school like I had. (Denial is such a wonderful thing.) I spent the rest of the night alternating between relief over her growth and worry about her development. But that was just the beginning.

Aside from being breech and delivered via C-section, Kaylee was healthy and everything appeared normal. As the months and typical landmarks rolled by, Jan began to notice that Kaylee wasn't verbalizing with words. She would make grunts and groans instead. She wasn't happy and cried a lot. Kaylee also had unusual patches of skin that were lighter than the surrounding areas.

With three children from a previous marriage, it was clear to Jan that something wasn't right. She asked their pediatrician about her concerns. In reply, the doctor told her not to worry about the lighter areas of skin.

When Kaylee was two years old, they went to Children's Hospital for a developmental evaluation. The professionals did a variety of assessments including giving Kaylee simple instructions and looking at different milestones. Jan thought Kaylee's problem was simply not talking and not accomplishing everything she needed to at her age.

Looking back, Jan didn't know what she anticipated as a result of the evaluation except for Kaylee perhaps needing extra therapy. Instead, the doctors determined that not only was Kaylee developmentally disabled (not delayed), she had tuberous sclerosis. Tuberous sclerosis causes benign tumors to grow in the brain and on other vital organs such as the kidneys, heart, eyes, lungs and skin. It commonly affects the central nervous system and results in a combination of symptoms including seizures, developmental delay, behavioral problems, and skin abnormalities.[xv]

As Jan put it, "I was in shock and in denial and sad to find out that she was disabled. That meant mental retardation. I had never heard of tuberous sclerosis and wondered how they found that. All of my hopes and dreams were shattered. It was really devastating. I thought I was prepared. We had gone in with a few questions but we came away with this."

Jan and her husband already had a vacation scheduled and weren't sure if they could go after the news. Because they had already paid money for the trip, they went. Jan said, "I wasn't sure I wanted to come back because I knew what I was going to face."

Lisa and Rick had two children and were working in a boy's home in Texas caring for and helping rebellious teenaged boys. Although Lisa was involved in ministry and another pregnancy came as a surprise, she quickly grew excited about having another baby.

Spencer was born 6 weeks early and was a big baby, already weighing close to 8 pounds. Lisa's worries about him being early were confirmed when Spencer's lungs collapsed. He had to be resuscitated and was given a lot of preventative antibiotics and other medications including a man-made lung surfactant.

Spencer pushed through the difficulties and after three weeks of being a very large preemie, was doing well. In fact, the doctors were amazed at how well he was doing and advancing. He was a great eater and a chubby, happy baby. On the other hand, Spencer had asthma for the first 6 months of his life.

Lisa and Rick knew that three kids and a houseful of 8 other boys was too much to handle, so they left the boys' home and moved to Fort Collins because they had heard it was a great place to raise a family and Rick's father had just moved there. Once in Fort Collins, Spencer's asthma went away because of the drier climate.

When Spencer was around 2, they began to notice a few minor problems. He had started walking late but not too terribly late. His speech started a little late as well but, since he was such a content baby, Lisa could explain that away.

By the time he turned three, their pediatrician told them it would be a good idea to get early intervention through the school system. The doctor did not give them a label or diagnosis but said that Spencer was a little delayed. The school system did their own testing and noticed some disability or late learning.

Around that same time, Spencer needed to have his immunizations. After he got them, he had a reaction and setback, losing all of his speech. Lisa knew there was something wrong and realized that his immune system couldn't handle certain things.

There were also problems at the preschool with Spencer sometimes screaming when he didn't understand. It was hard for teachers to like him because he acted out a lot. Lisa and Rick prayed that teachers would fall in love with Spencer and see past his behaviors. A couple of weeks later, one teacher told them, "I'm really falling in love with your son. I want to spend some extra time figuring him out."

Over the course of two years in preschool, Spencer advanced and was accepted. Once he felt accepted in the environment, he did very well and was their shining star. Yet, during that time, it was also recognized that he had a high-functioning autistic mentality and that label was added.

In the meantime, when Spencer was 4 years old, Jesse was born. He was a surprise to the family because, while they had always talked about having four children, with Spencer's issues they thought that maybe three kids was all that they could handle. Jesse was a great child for the first year. Lisa said he was a blessing and a gift because Spencer now could experience being the older brother.

As Jesse grew, they started to see him think and act like Spencer. "Is he mimicking what Spencer is doing or is this real? Does he think this way?" Lisa thought. Through a process of time and in a different way, it was determined that Jesse was also on the autism spectrum with Asberger's syndrome. Jesse was social and communicated very well but had emotional highs and lows. The boys thought the same way and processed information similarly. Instead of just one autistic child, Lisa and Rick now had two very different yet similar children.

Sherilyn felt that her pregnancy was normal except that she was sick for nine months. It was difficult being sick every day and she was anxious for it to be over. When the baby was full term, her doctor wanted to induce labor. Sherilyn and her husband agreed since it fell on his day off from work.

Sherilyn's labor was induced and she was in labor for seven or eight hours. Difficult contractions came every one or two minutes but nothing really happened. The doctor initially said that if her water didn't break, she would be sent home because the baby wasn't ready to come. The hospital was busy that day with every room filled and even two women delivering in the hall. Suddenly, the doctor walked in around noon and, despite what he had said earlier, broke her water. Later, Sherilyn wondered if she should have gone home instead.

Sherilyn then had another 14 hours of hard contractions. The staff was so busy they didn't have time to carefully monitor the screens like they would have with a fewer number of patients. If they had, they would have noticed that the baby's heart rate went down every time she had a contraction. The cord was wrapped two and a half times around his neck and every time she had a contraction, it was cutting off the blood supply and oxygen to his brain. As the delivery progressed, instead of doing a c-section, the doctor used forceps to deliver David.

David was about two to three weeks premature physically. His lungs were premature. He had yellow jaundice and his eyes were crooked. He was put in intensive care and needed several blood transfusions. He hadn't been ready to be born. After 5 or 6 days, doctors said his lungs were now developed so he could be on his own and David was finally sent home.

Every time Sherilyn changed his diaper it was very hard to hold his legs down. David wanted to curl them up, because his muscles were so tight. Being a young mother with her first baby, Sherilyn didn't realize that this was not normal.

When David was 6 to 8 months old, Sherilyn's sister came for a visit. She was the first one who said, "I don't want to hurt your feeling but, besides just having a lazy eye, this isn't normal. His little legs are supposed to lay down and relax when you are changing his diaper." David was also stiff on his left side.

Sherilyn began to take him to a program where, at nine months of age, they diagnosed him with mild cerebral palsy. He had been wearing a patch all the time to correct his lazy eye. That had been downplayed at the hospital with the statement, "If he just wears this patch for six months, that will straighten out."

Looking back, Sherilyn saw that the lazy eye was part of the cerebral palsy and not having the muscle coordination for both eyes to track together. She also realized that the doctors at the hospital didn't want to say, "We think your child has some physical problems" because she would have asked, "Why is that?" The hospital would have had to answer for breaking her water contrary to the doctor's earlier decision and the lack of monitoring during labor. Instead, David had been born early after 23 hours of oxygen-deprivation during contractions.

Linda and Keith sent their 8-year-old son, Thom, to spend time with his paternal grandparents in Nebraska. Thom was looking forward to his special time with his grandparents since his brother and sister had spent the previous summer with them.

The last few months had been stressful. Thom often had to run to make it to the bathroom. Linda and Keith gave him a hard time about waiting until the last minute to go, but the only solution to the problem was a cart blanche "go when you need to go" permission from his teacher.

On the long trip in the car from California to Nebraska, Linda read aloud from one of the Chronicles of Narnia books. Thom was uncomfortable and had to recline on a pillow to listen. Often, they had to make a hurried stop for Thom to use the bathroom.

When Linda and Keith left him with his grandparents, they encouraged them to keep a close eye on Thom. About two weeks after they arrived back home in California, they received a frantic call from Keith's parents. Over the weekend, Thom's stomach was hard so they had taken him to the doctor. The doctor had given Thom an enema and sent him home. When that did not work, they tried further treatment and eventually put him in the hospital.

The doctors eventually found an enlarged lymph node under Thom's arm and further testing revealed he possibly had cancer. Since Thom needed treatment immediately, he would be flying home to his parents the next day.

Linda said, "We met him at the airport and drove directly to the Los Angeles Children's Hospital where he was admitted. It was a shock to see him. The happy bouncing boy we knew was in a wheelchair and clearly not doing well. We quickly found that the chair was not needed and, with a little encouragement, he became the happy boy we had left in Nebraska. However, he did not have his full bounce."

"We were sure this was just a trial and there was an end in sight. It turned out not to be a short-lived trial. We went to a conference with the doctors the next day and learned Thom had cancer. We did not realize the complete truth of their statement. We thought it was just a minor hurdle."

During the next few weeks, the doctors did a battery of different tests on Thom and developed a plan to combat the disease. Thom had a little-known cancer simply called "undifferentiated adult cancer" that never went into any of his organs but lingered in his abdominal cavity. Linda said, "It had only been found in two other adults and treated without much success since both died."

Roxanne and Tony had four years of infertility treatments before they learned they were pregnant. Because of Roxanne's age, they were considered a high-risk pregnancy. Then, just six months after losing the baby girl they were trying to adopt to SIDS, Roxanne had a miscarriage.

When she found out she was pregnant again, Roxanne feared another miscarriage. Since her miscarriage happened right after hearing the baby's heartbeat and starting to wear maternity clothes, she didn't pull out the maternity clothes until well into the fifth month. "I wasn't trying to be superstitious, but I was. I thought that if I put the maternity clothes on I'd lose the baby. It was the shortest pregnancy on record because he came almost 7 weeks early. I never got to the point of being sick of being pregnant!"

Roxanne went into early labor at 32 ½ weeks and her water broke. When the doctor saw her, he said they needed to get through the 33rd week for lung development if possible and was going to put her on medication to control the labor. When the womb became a less healthy environment for the baby than the neonatal intensive care unit (NICU), then they would have the baby. On the other hand, there was a nurse telling Roxanne, "You need to have that baby right now. You're asking for infection and all kinds of trouble. You'll live to regret it if you don't."

All Roxanne could do was trust the doctor who had followed her throughout her pregnancy. Since she needed to be on bed rest but not necessarily in the hospital, Roxanne was eager to head home where her sister was coming to visit. But, before she could be discharged, nurses caught a problem on the monitor. Suddenly plans changed and her husband Tony was called to come in with the words, "Today is your baby's birth day."

Roxanne thought, "Wait, this is almost 7 weeks early." She was also panicked about needing an emergency c-section. At that point, Roxanne had to be given medication to induce labor and began to have horrendous and intense back labor. For whatever reason, she couldn't have any pain medications. In the course of the labor, Roxanne's sister kept watching the heart monitor dropping. Roxanne only got to push twice before forceps were used to bring Rob onto the scene.

Rob was only five and a half pounds, but he had a big head. He was immediately rushed to the corner where three pediatricians began working on him. There wasn't a cry. There was nothing and they rushed him out of the room. Tony followed them to the nursery where Rob was resuscitated. His apgar scores were low but the nurses told Tony that Rob was excellent weight for a baby almost 7 weeks early. "He's going to be fine." Tony kept arguing, "But …" and the nurses argued back, "No buts. We've got an excellent ICU. We're going to keep him on oxygen today and probably will be able to take him off tomorrow. He's going to need the billi lights but our ICU is nationally known. He's going to be fine."

The next morning, Roxanne went to the ICU to see him. There were bells and whistles going off and three-pound babies everywhere. A man walked up to Roxanne and said, "Do you have any questions?"

As a practicing speech pathologist, Roxanne was supposed to know all of the infant reflexes but hadn't been working in that area for some time. Plus, they had missed all of their Lamaze classes because Rob was born early. Looking down at Rob under the lights, covered up and taped down and not moving, Roxanne said, "I need a refresher course on the reflexes. Does he have the reflexes he is supposed to have?"

"Well, actually we're questioning that too. We're having him tested for Down syndrome," the man replied.

And that is how Roxanne found out. All she could think was "No, no, no. That's not how I'm supposed to find out. I'm supposed to be in my hospital room and my husband is supposed to be beside me. There's supposed to be a social worker there with the doctor saying we have these concerns and would like to have him tested." Instead, twelve hours after Rob was born, Roxanne was standing all alone beside an isolette. "What leads you to that conclusion?" she asked and began to argue with the doctor about whether Rob's ears were lower set or not.

Somehow, Roxanne got back to her room. Tony came in, flying high and excited about the baby. Now that Rob had arrived and was being taken care of, Tony could schedule a time to fly out to see his father. Tony's father had just been diagnosed with pancreatic cancer and given seven weeks to live, which would have coincided with the baby's due date.

Instead, Roxanne had to tell him they couldn't schedule the trip quite yet and had to break the news about Rob. Tony pulled his military connections and within 30 minutes the room was filled with the head geneticist, the developmental pediatrician, the social worker and about five other people prepared to answer whatever questions they had. But, nobody ever apologized for Roxanne's getting the news the way she had.

Tony decided that they weren't going to tell people about the possibility of something being wrong until they got test results back and knew for sure. So, it became a deep dark secret.

A few hours later, a nurse came in and said, "You look a little down. What is the problem? You've got your baby. Why are you upset?"

Roxanne wanted to say, "Sweetheart, I was on my way home yesterday. I am now the mother of a possibly handicapped child and he's almost 7 weeks early. This was not on my schedule." Instead, because she couldn't say anything about the Downs, Roxanne did say what she could, "I've been hit pretty hard the last twelve hours and I'm trying to deal with it. He has beta strep."

"Oh, that beta strep," the nurse replied. "That is so awful. The baby's are doing okay and then they crash and they die."

Roxanne looked at the nurse. "I don't need to hear that."

"Actually," she replied, "it's the nurses' responsibility because a lot of times the doctors don't give you all the information that you need, so we feel obligated to make sure that you understand the severity."

"My husband and I ask hundreds more questions than most of your patients. We have doctors that we trust. We have not lacked information. When I'm dealing with everything that I have dealt with this last 12 hours, I don't need you on top of that to send the message that my child might die any minute now." The nurse just sputtered and left. When Tony found out about it, he barred that nurse from ever coming back.

While they were waiting to find out what the diagnosis was, Rob's weight was being carefully monitored. Roxanne would pump and let him drink from a bottle instead of nursing because it was easier. The daily weight check came at midnight, so she would feed him right before midnight and hope he hadn't lost even an ounce or else she couldn't nurse him at all the next day. Rob was having muscular issues with chewing, sucking and swallowing plus, as a preemie, nursing was difficult. Having to alternate between nursing and bottle feeding was both confusing and frustrating.

Rob had to stay in the hospital to finish the 10-day course of IV antibiotics for beta strep so Roxanne stayed with Rob while Tony took the opportunity to fly to see his father. At the end of that ten days, they learned that Rob had mosaic Down syndrome which occurs in 1-2% of the Downs population.[xvi] Rob's chromosome karyotype revealed that 40% of his cells had the extra chromosome causing Down syndrome while the rest were normal. The condition was so rare that most of the doctors Roxanne worked with had only seen 2 mosaics in their entire careers.

Mosaicism can occur with any syndrome and there is a large range of affectedness. Some mosaic Downs children have symptoms as involved or more involved than a high functioning Downs child, while, in other cases, you wouldn't even realize that anything was wrong. It all depended on if the affected cells were in the brain or the big toe.

Rob had a simian crease, lower set ears and a wider set space between his big toe and second toe. He had 8 sets of PE (pressure-equalization) tubes put in his ears through the years. He had low muscle tone, but Roxanne now believes that was more due to his being premature since he is currently in a low-average range. Rob was also hyper-flexible and could put both legs behind his neck and fold up like a pretzel, even at the age of 16.

Due to complications delivering my second child, I spent three days in the ICU and received five units of blood. So, when we found out we were expecting a third baby, my doctors monitored my platelet counts diligently. As the counts dropped drastically and then leveled off as the due date approached, we scheduled an amniocentesis for the day before Thanksgiving and a c-section delivery for that Friday assuming the test results were good. Bags of platelets were on standby from a nearby hospital just in case they were needed. It was the safest way to handle my complications and yet assure that our baby boy would be fully developed.

On Tuesday, I went into labor on my own, two and a half weeks before my official due date. My in-laws came to pick up Anna and Luke while my husband and I timed contractions. When we arrived at the hospital later that night, blood was quickly drawn for another platelet count while the operating room was prepared for my delivery. Those test results showed yet another dangerous dip in my platelet count. Had we waited until Friday as scheduled, the levels could have been life threatening again. Instead, God brought our baby boy early to save my life.

Joel didn't fare as well. At first he was placed under an oxygen hood and then later on a nasal c-pap device to help inflate his lungs. He was working so hard to breathe that his entire chest retracted with every breath. By early Thursday (Thanksgiving) morning, Joel had to be put on a respirator and was given a surfactant medication to keep the inside of his lungs from sticking to itself. Since our local hospital did not have the staff to monitor him, Joel and his dad rode in an ambulance to Children's Hospital in Denver early Thanksgiving Day while I stayed behind in the hospital.

That evening, my parents drove up to Loveland to pick me up. After a quick stop at our house to pack an overnight bag, we headed to Children's Hospital to see Joel and pick up Clint. Because of a flu epidemic, I had to put on a gown, mask, hair covering and gloves before I could be wheeled in to the NICU (I had just had abdominal surgery and couldn't walk that far yet) to see my baby. The numerous tubes coming out of Joel were mind-boggling.

Over the next week, we juggled getting two kids back to school and Clint back to work while I spent time at the hospital with Joel. He made progress and was off the respirator by late Friday night – only to be put back on Saturday morning. Tests revealed that his right lung was full of fluid leaking from the central IV line. Once his lung was drained with a giant needle and the IV line moved, he recovered quickly. He eventually was able to go home without oxygen and thrived.

As a baby, he seemed to have sensitive skin. He would have a reaction whenever he touched his Dad's shirt after Dad had helped work with the horses at Grandma and Grandpa's acreage. As a toddler, there were times his eyes would get red and his voice would sound scratchy if he had been playing in the barn at the grandparents' home.

The summer he was two, Joel was watching Anna at her therapeutic horseback-riding lesson and was playing with some toys on the floor of the waiting room. Within a matter of minutes, he was whimpering and sitting in my lap. Lifting his shirt, I noticed red spots growing on his chest and he began to breathe faster. I took him to the car, removed his clothes and washed him off with wet wipes from the diaper bag. Soon, the spots and discomfort disappeared. I realized he was allergic to horses or hay and thought of my own Sudafed days because of hay fever. It must run in the family, I thought.

In October, before he turned three, Joel got a cold. He was coughing a lot in the middle of the night and so I put him in bed with me. By morning, after getting the other kids off to school, I noticed that he was wheezing as he breathed. Lifting his shirt, I saw the same chest retractions that he'd had at birth and I panicked. A quick call to the doctor and we got right in. They immediately gave him albuterol in a nebulizer and within minutes, Joel was a totally different child. The doctor called it "viral-induced asthma" but said it did not mean that he had asthma – just that he had asthma-like symptoms with this viral illness and we would treat it the same as asthma. We went home with a prescription for more albuterol, a medication that dilates the bronchial tubes, and had a nebulizer machine delivered.

Four weeks later, Joel had another cold with the same difficulty breathing. But this time the effect of the albuterol didn't last more than an hour. Another trip to the doctor and we added an anti-inflammatory steroid medication to the nebulizer treatments. With both medications and the machine at home, I felt confident that I could handle another illness-related episode. Several more colds over the winter did not result in breathing issues and I felt we were past it.

In March, at age 3 ½, Joel spent the night at Grandma and Grandpa's house like he had many times before. The next morning, he was crying for me and having a hard time breathing. They called their neighbor, a nurse, who brought her stethoscope over and listened to his lungs crackle and watched his chest retracting. By the time I got there, intending to take him home for a nebulizer treatment, this nurse was already giving him a treatment because her daughter had similar issues. It happened again the next time he spent the night at Grandma's.

By now, I knew that there was something at their house that was causing him to have an asthma reaction. I pursued a referral to an allergy and asthma doctor. In May, Joel was tested for allergies and we learned that he was allergic to dogs, cats, horses and locust trees. All of these were at the grandparent's house and explained his problems if he spent time there. The doctor gave us prescriptions for allergy and asthma medications as well as a folder of information.

Since I had already figured out what was wrong, it was easier to hear the doctor say the words confirming what I already thought. The hard part came when I realized this might be a lifelong problem for Joel and that he might not outgrow it as he got older. Having already lived with Anna's learning and behavior issues for ten years by this point, a problem that could be treated with regular medications seemed relatively easy to live with.

Everything was typical when Lucas was born except that Lori had to stop pushing for a minute or two because the cord was around his neck. As he grew, Lucas went from rocking back and forth like babies do to an army commando crawl. He didn't do the typical crawling pattern on hands and knees until after he started walking at a year and then came back to it.

Looking back through his baby books, Lori had written that he had said "Mama" and "Dada." While she thought that he had, she later wondered if he was just playing with consonants and babbling. Eventually, he started to get some words. He'd play peek-a-boo and make eye contact with people. He could jump and bounce for hours in the Johnny Jumper hanging in the doorway.

His first year had been pretty normal. But then, suddenly, Lucas started crying at noises. Lori used to be able to vacuum under his crib and it didn't affect him at all, but now he cried. There were other things that were just a little bit different and Lori couldn't quite put her finger on what was wrong. She had a niece born the same day as Lucas who was practically born talking. Lori tried not to compare them. People would say, "You know boys are slower and it's okay." The doctor said, "Everything's fine. Don't worry. He'll catch up. Some are just different."

Then, when Lucas was 18-months-old, Lori went on a trip to be in a wedding. When she came back, her family came to greet her at the airport and Lucas walked right by her. Lori thought he was just really mad at her and said so to the other adults who were there. But, there was something that made the hair on her neck stand up and she thought, "Something is just not right." She wasn't ready to admit it out loud but it seemed like Lucas had withdrawn.

At age two, the few words Lucas had learned began to disappear and he started to do odd things. While Lori took a class, Lucas went to a daycare at the college. The workers at the daycare said, "You know, we're wondering if there's something wrong with his hearing because we can bang pans behind him and he doesn't even move." And yet, Lori knew he could hear because Barney would come on the TV and he would race off. He seemed to block out loud noises.

Lucas would spin objects. He would take his plate on his high chair, make it spin and be fascinated. He would go around flushing toilets because the spinning water would fascinate him. All along, his pediatrician said, "Don't worry about it. It's okay." But it was not okay to Lori that Lucas wasn't talking more.

The workers at the daycare recommended that the developmental center for children aged birth to three could help Lucas get caught up because of his delays. Lori remembered her husband saying, "It's okay. We'll just get him caught up. Nobody ever needs to know that he was delayed."

Lori remembered talking to the school psychologist one day when Lucas began to flap his hands excitedly. The psychologist asked if Lucas did that often. Lori said, "Yeah, he gets really excited and he just flaps with his hands. Isn't that funny?"

The psychologist said, "Well, sometimes kids with autism …" That was the first time Lori heard the word autism and Lucas mentioned together. Her only point of reference with autism was the movie "Rain Man." She was devastated and thought, "How could you even imply that? How dare you say that?"

With their pediatrician still not believing anything was wrong, they went to Children's Hospital at the encouragement of the developmental center staff. Lucas was officially diagnosed with autism the day after his 3rd birthday party.

Adam was an avid ice hockey player. He volunteered teaching younger kids to skate and hit the puck and earned a spot in an expensive ice hockey camp. The camp schedule would be filled with hard knocks, aggressive play and bodies slamming into the boards. The players would have conditioning workouts and then get on the ice to see who was the toughest and determine who would make the team the following week.

In June, after his freshman year of high school, Adam complained of a headache one day and simply forgot about the start of his hockey camp. On Tuesday, Adam went to work and his coach asked him where he had been because the camp had started. He told his coach that he had forgotten and would be there on Wednesday. When he came home from work, Adam told his mother, Sherilyn, that he had forgotten about the camp and he was going to bed because he had a headache. Adam was not a complainer and, looking back, Sherilyn said she should have known he was feeling worse than he said.

In the morning, Adam decided he felt good enough to go to the hockey camp. However, he called right after Sherilyn got back home from taking him saying he didn't feel like staying after doing the exercises and asked her to come back and pick him up. So, Sherilyn brought him home. On Thursday, he still didn't feel like going. By Friday of that week, Adam felt like going but was worried because he wasn't in shape and was far behind the other players. He decided to just write it off while his mother bit her tongue.

On Saturday, Grandpa came to visit and three generations went out to shoot shotguns while Sherilyn went along to watch. Adam was physically dragging and got frustrated and mad when he couldn't hit the targets. Instead of shooting, he spent the rest of the day walking around with Sherilyn.

Sunday, Sherilyn drove Adam and a friend to a church camp in Nebraska. On Wednesday, she got a phone call from Adam saying that he wasn't feeling well and that he wanted her to bring him some Tylenol. "Tylenol would be nice. Happy Birthday Mom. But can you bring me some Tylenol? And, oh, by the way, you know the whites of my eyes, they are starting to turn green. And Chad says I look like a lizard." Adam had a keen sense of humor and used exaggeration and wit in his humor so Sherilyn was sure that he was exaggerating. "My face is turning yellow. I'm really not feeling well and I'm kinda tired." Sherilyn says they were laughing since he now said he'd had the headache for six weeks instead of six days. Everything was exaggerated.

Still, she called the nurse and their doctor and asked what to do since it sounded like Adam might have jaundice. They told her not to worry and to bring him in when he got home.

On Thursday, Adam still had a headache but he wasn't feeling worse. Sherilyn still had the camp staff take him to the hospital in nearby North Platte. Within an hour, the doctor called her. "We've got the results back from Adam's blood tests and we cannot find any platelets in his blood system. We think he has a case of acute leukemia. I will not release him from this hospital because he could die if he bumps his knee and starts bleeding. If there is a weak spot in his body somewhere and he starts bleeding internally, we won't be able to pump the blood into his body fast enough and he will bleed to death."

The doctor was blunt with Sherilyn on the phone and held nothing back about the seriousness of Adam's condition. In fact, he said, "We're going to send him to Denver with Flight for Life because I'm not sure he can live through a five hour ambulance ride." Adam thought he only had three days to live.

Sherilyn said, "My knees just gave out from where I was standing and I sank into the chair beside the desk. I somehow answered the questions of where do I want you to send him, what do you suggest, Children's Hospital, okay. Yes I give permission for this. I give permission for that. What is your phone number? I got his phone number and then I hung up. I just put my head down to pray. And bawl."

Each of these families received unexpected news about their children and learned life wouldn't be the same. But, initial pucker aside, they still had to get the juice out of the lemons. And that wouldn't be easy either.

In Your Kitchen

1. For each of the stories above, how do you think you would have reacted?

2. Find your list of lemons from Chapter 1. Next to each lemon listed, rank on a scale of 1 (barely) to 10 (severe pucker) how extreme your reaction was.

3. Why were some lemons worse than others?

4. Pick one of your lemons as an example and write it briefly as a story, revealing the events leading up to the bad news and your resulting emotions.

3 - JUICING LEMONS

Barbara Gill, the mother of a child with Down syndrome, wrote, "For most of us the beginning is a traumatic and wrenching experience. Our insides are torn by such shock, grief, fear, and sense of loss that it feels like death. Our very identity comes under assault as on every side our assumptions and expectations are turned on their heads. At all the points where we touch the outside world – relating to our family and friends, interacting with medical and social service systems, going out in public – we are stretched and challenged. The whole shape of our selves and our lives is being pulled into a new form."[xvii]

To make lemonade, you need lemon juice, not lemons. So, how do you separate the juice from the rest of the lemon? It happens by a process that rips the guts of the lemon to shreds as it is cut, upended, squeezed and twisted under pressure over a ridged cone known as a citrus reamer or juicer. It continues with the second lemon half and the next lemon and the next until enough juice is gathered.

Like the process of juicing a lemon, we experience a wide variety of emotions. We can feel as though our hearts are being ripped out. Everything has turned upside down. We are being squeezed under pressure. We are being rubbed the wrong way. Just when we think the pain might be over, it hits again.

As Christians, we sometimes think that our feelings of anger, fear, guilt, depression and despair are wrong. But God gave us our feelings. They are normal and it is okay to feel. Even Jesus, God in the flesh, experienced feelings of sadness when He wept at the death of a friend, anger when he overturned tables in the Temple and agony in the garden when he faced the coming pain.

Through the emotional juicing process we may feel disconnected from society and from the normal flow of our lives. Our limited past experiences may only offer negative images of what lies ahead. Sherilyn's mother-in-law suffered five years with leukemia before dying just four months before Sherilyn's son, Adam, was diagnosed with leukemia. Sherilyn grew up in the generation where if someone had leukemia, they died because there weren't any cures. When she heard that her son had leukemia, there were only two facts in her mind. Leukemia is cancer and you die from it. It was not part of her life and therefore she had no idea that modern day research had brought the odds of recovery up dramatically.

Without a useful history to give a clear picture of the future, we are filled with fear. Questions flood our minds: "How serious is this?" "Will she have friends?" "What will happen to my life?" "What will happen to her?"

While doctors can provide medication to ease the pain of childbirth, I wish there was something to erase the feelings of agony and sorrow. As if those emotions weren't enough, then we start spreading the news to family and friends and bear the brunt of their reactions. It's easy to take on their pain as well as our own, as if we are somehow responsible.

It is normal to be afraid and to feel alone in your pain. But you are not the only one to feel this way. Your emotions are valid and normal. You are understood, if not by society, by the millions of other mothers, fathers and caretakers around the world. There is no right way to react. There is only your way.

We don't think that we can survive these emotions or handle the tasks ahead, but we will. We have a child to care for and duties that absorb our attention. We go forward, step by step, to meet the demands of the day. Our lives are not destroyed but bent in a new direction. Our lives are not over but dramatically reshaped.

People say that children change your life forever. When one of your children has a disability, this sentiment sounds like a huge understatement. When Anna was diagnosed, I realized we were on the most life-changing and challenging journey I'd ever experienced.

We are on a journey we didn't plan on taking. One mother of a child with Down syndrome described it as planning a trip to Italy and finding that the plane instead landed in Holland. Another mother said their trip led them across deserts, valleys and mountains when their itinerary was set for Orlando. The unexpected destination takes getting used to as we abandon our previous plans.

So, in order to make lemonade, we must get the juice out of the lemons through an often life-changing and painful process. Experts call the resulting vast range of emotion the grief process. Grieving is a normal and necessary step in our journey.

Grief is a personal and emotional reaction to a significant loss, usually the death of a loved one or being involved in a tragedy. But it is not only physical loss that brings grieving. We can also grieve the loss of dreams, hopes and expectations – the loss of what might have been.

Those with children born with disabilities have to give up their fantasy of a perfect baby. We grieve the loss of a dream and our previous expectations. Grieving the loss of the baby we were expecting does not mean we are ungrateful for the baby we were given. On the other hand, parents whose children become disabled due to an accident, illness or progressive disease grieve for a very real child.

Grief is an individual experience. No two people will experience or express grief in exactly the same way and there is no right way to behave when grieving. Despite the personal nature of grief, there are a number of general stages that most people pass through on the road to accepting a significant loss. These basic stages include shock, denial, anger, guilt, and depression. We get to the other side of our grief in the only way possible: by going through it.

Let's take a closer look at each of these emotional stages.

Shock happens when our idealistic dreams are crushed and we discover that our child is unhealthy or handicapped in some way. It is a stage often characterized by feelings of numbness or disbelief. Some parents feel paralyzed, distant or disconnected from the reality of their situation. The parents in the last chapter experienced this puckering shock.

For Lori, it was another blow at an already tough time in her life. Her husband had just lost his job and Lucas was going to a special school to help get him caught up. Then Lori delivered a newborn baby weighing 9 pounds 12 ounces and broke her tailbone during the delivery. Already emotionally spent and weepy, she then learned that Lucas had autism. "It was all at once and quite hard. It was devastating."

Roxanne experienced the grief process firsthand before Rob was even born. After losing the daughter they were adopting to SIDS, Roxanne then miscarried after 4 years of infertility treatments. "When I miscarried, I subconsciously took it as I'm still in the process of getting over a child so the miscarriage can't have as much weight. I discounted the grief I went through until we went to a living Christmas program. Mary and Joseph came out with baby Jesus and I was in histrionics trying to figure out how to get out of the auditorium."

Roxanne said, "It hadn't hit me until I was sitting there and watched them walk in how different this Christmas would have been if I had a nine month old baby and I was pregnant. Instead I was sitting there less than a month after a miscarriage with no baby, no adoption in the works and no great chance that I was going to be able to get pregnant again." Roxanne, as a speech pathologist, had led workshops on grief and the chronic grief of parents of children with disabilities but it didn't hit home until they had lost Sunni Anne and then had the miscarriage.

For Lisa, the truth finally sank in after reading an article in Time magazine that described autism. There were a few key points that stuck in Lisa's mind. One of them was "They'll never understand relationships." Another was "They will float around in society but never have the comprehension that we have." While there was a lot of helpful information in the article, Lisa was stunned by the few negative statements and didn't look at the rest. "It absorbed into me and I realized the truth. It hit me that this was huge and bigger than I thought. I don't think I can conquer this."

Denial, the next stage, is an attempt to protect us from the shock by retreating. We don't believe this is happening, and, like removing our hand from the fire, our minds seek to remove us from the source of pain as quickly as possible. Denial does serve a purpose by providing temporary protection from a hostile environment.

In its simplest form, denial is an attempt to distance ourselves from pain. We try to ease our anxiety by twisting our attention to something else. We make excuses for our child's behavior or symptoms. We remind ourselves that doctors sometimes make mistakes. We throw ourselves into other activities or work in order to escape the situation at home.

How long we spend in denial depends on the individual.

Bombarded by the diagnosis of Lucas' autism, Lori first went into denial and then quickly moved on. Meanwhile, the denial stage for her husband lasted months.

Some parents find themselves in extended denial. They continue to dispute a child's diagnosis even after a second opinion. They resist enrolling the child in a special-needs program despite the advice of a specialist. They ignore major developmental delays or abnormal behaviors. For some, professional counseling may be needed to move beyond this stage. For most, moving beyond denial is just another hurdle on the road.

When Noah was three, Shannon assumed that his lack of speech was because he had a very high palette. Noah was still young and some typical kids don't start speaking until later. He was still in the window of typical development and she was willing to wait for his speech to come. When a speech therapist told them Noah had dyspraxia dysarthria, Shannon didn't know what that was. "I was in a fog. I heard all this information like he may not speak, he may not be intelligible, it may not happen. I'm like 'Oh, okay,' but it didn't really register until I got home and talked to Ray. Then I thought, 'Whoa. He may never speak.'"

Anger may seem to be an unhealthy emotion but it marks the beginning of healing. In the short term, anger offers protection from our emotional trauma.

When we feel anxious, helpless, or overwhelmed by a situation, anger comes to the rescue. Not only does it neutralize the debilitating worry for a while, it also restores a semblance of power and authority when we need it the most.

It's okay to be angry. To be angry that my child is suffering. And to be angry with the people who gawk and stare.

Being told that we shouldn't be angry doesn't make sense. Anger is both a natural and normal response when our expectations aren't met. We tend to believe that things should go our way all of the time. Intellectually, we know that is neither true nor realistic but we are still shocked when bad things happen to good people. We need to recognize and accept that things go wrong in life. After all, Jesus said that we would have trouble in this world.[xviii]

Created in God's image, we have emotions and one of those emotions is anger. Like all of God's gifts, anger has tremendous potential for good. We can choose to express our anger in ways that help or in ways that hinder. In ways that build or in ways that destroy. Often, facing our anger and allowing ourselves to feel are the first steps in resolving anger.

There are two anger responses when things don't go our way. The first is a righteous anger that compels us to make a difference in the situation. This type of response was demonstrated through the civil rights movement. The other type of anger can causes us to do foolish things that hurt others and ourselves. Outrage because of the situation can be directed toward our child, our spouse, other family members, professionals, God or anyone else we can find to lash out at. Lashing out at others releases the immediate pressure but the resulting consequences may make the situation worse.

There is a moment between the event and my reaction. In that moment, I have a choice to make. No one can *make* me angry unless I choose that response. I can, in that moment of decision, try to count to 100 (twice if necessary) before responding instead of reacting.

But, if I'm feeling helpless in a situation, I might still lose control with an outburst of anger. Some days, all it takes is one more thing to send me over the edge. If you have lost it today, acknowledge it. Forgive yourself and apologize to your child and family. Tomorrow is a new day and you can begin again.

One of the side effects of anger is displacement where we shift the focus of our anger from its original target onto another object or person less threatening or more convenient. Some parents enter into long disputes with schools or doctors. They may become overzealous in their attempts to "save" their child and set impossible goals for the child's teacher or therapists to achieve. Other parents direct their anger toward finding a cure, obtaining funding for research or enacting legislation.

Jan was a very busy lady trying to do all of the right things. She was so busy handling things that she didn't realize that she was losing herself. Because Kaylee was the first child on her husband's side of the family, Jan thought that everyone would be holding her and that Kaylee would be loved. That didn't turn out to be true. In fact, her husband worked just down the street with his father and chose not to come home for lunch. Jan felt like she was all alone taking care of Kaylee and began to feel sorry for herself. "I was very, very angry and my anger turned into a lot of bitterness and ire and rage. I sought other fixes just to be able to feel something. I grew tired of being angry all the time."

If you feel angry about your lemon situation, you are not alone.

Guilt, another emotion in the juicing process, happens when we begin to wonder if we did something to cause our child's illness or condition or if we didn't do something to prevent it. Blaming God, others or yourself is a natural reaction to finding out your child has a disability or disease. We want answers to our questions: What caused this? Who is to blame?

After the initial shock and anger wear off, a parent begins an internal argument. If only I hadn't _____, this wouldn't be happening. If only the doctors had _____. If only I had known, I would have _____. If only I'd studied our family's medical history. If only. We cannot go back and change the past.

After finding out her son David had cerebral palsy, Sherilyn faced the guilt factor because it was their decision to go ahead and induce the delivery, not knowing that their baby wasn't ready to be born. Many people around them also encouraged them to sue the hospital for negligence. Somebody else needed to take the blame.

We feel like we need to blame something or somebody.

Maybe I can't blame my spouse for the illness, but I can point out their other faults. Somehow, I have to get this emotion out of me and it is convenient to place it on somebody else. However, blaming another or ourselves punishes us in a way we do not deserve.

Jan and her husband Cary had DNA testing done on themselves to find the source of Kaylee's tuberous sclerosis. Jan said, "I was so sure that Cary passed it on. That would give me a great excuse to blame somebody." Cary's mother had passed away from a giant cell astrocytoma brain tumor – the same type of tumor that can develop in individuals with tuberous sclerosis. It seemed logical to assume that Kaylee's condition came from Cary's side of the family. Instead, they found out that it was caused by a new mutation and the blame had nowhere to go.

Feelings of guilt can arise from a sense of failure and regret. Some parents try to compensate for this guilt by working tirelessly on their child's educational and therapeutic needs or by making the child the family's number-one priority at all times. Ironically, this focused dedication may lead to more feelings of guilt when we realize our child is not improving or that the needs of the rest of the family are being neglected.

Feelings of guilt can also arise when we experience acts of prejudice toward our child and they hurt and anger us. As a result, we may feel guilt, remorse and regret over the way we treated people with disabilities in the past. We understand prejudice from both sides now.

You might even feel ashamed of your child and then feel guilty that you were ashamed. Sherilyn said, "Most moms don't want to talk about this, but there is the factor that you might be ashamed of your child. Everybody that has a baby wants the baby to be cute and wants people to walk up and say, 'What a cute little baby.' They're not going to say that about a baby whose eyes are looking in different directions and his left side is stiff. Within a few minutes, you notice that this baby has problems. People relate differently and become very uncomfortable. It puts you in an awkward situation no matter who you are around."

Just because the thought comes or you are embarrassed or you wish that your baby could be like every other baby – that's not horrible. Part of that wish is for the baby. But then, a big part of that wish is for yourself! This is your life that was interrupted and the years of surgeries, therapy and special schools are years that you will never recapture. And then you feel guilty for feeling that way.

For some, the emotions involved develop into depression. Depression can be defined as a prolonged feeling of intense sadness that can be accompanied by feelings of worthlessness, inadequacy and lethargy. It is an experience that can come when something we love or treasure is taken away. Depression is amplified by the sleep deprivation common when we are busy dealing with the emotional upheaval and various issues involved with a child with special needs.

As hard as we try to lift our spirits, our thoughts and emotions won't cooperate. We know that we have a lot to be thankful for, but emotions know no logic. Sleep becomes unpredictable. Fear of the future surprises us at awkward times and tears flow freely. The day-to-day routines of family life suffer as we become more depressed and exhausted. We may even wonder if we're a disappointment to God since we can't seem to conquer the blues.

Jan's emotional anguish over Kaylee's condition led to years of trying to find ways to escape. She felt ashamed and lonely. "I didn't want to live, but I couldn't kill myself. I didn't have the guts to do it and I could hear of voices of my children saying 'We would miss her.' It was a deep dark secret. I could just cry now because there was so much pain. It was horrible and empty and deep and dark and nobody was throwing me a rope. I felt like I was on an island and all alone."

For Lori, she thought that as a mom she was supposed to be the strong one. Others would say, "I don't know how you can do it." But Lori would go cry in the shower. "I would go in there and cry. I would wonder what was going to happen or if he was ever going to have friends. And then come out and be back to being Mom." She would hide her sorrow in the shower and then put on her Mom face.

Like juicing a lemon, the sour experiences in our lives cause us to feel upended, twisted under pressure and our insides are ripped out in a flow of emotion that includes shock, grief, denial, anger, guilt and depression. We may feel like a hollow shell of ourselves. Unfortunately, there is more juicing to be done.

In Your Kitchen

1. List the emotions you have experienced associated with the lemons you listed in Chapter 1.

2. Did you progress through the stages in order or skip around?

3. Was there an emotion that seemed to affect you more than others? Why?

4 - MORE JUICING

To juice a lemon, you cut it in half. Taking one half, you upend it over the rough surface of a juicer and twist it under pressure until the juice is out. Are you done? No, there is the other half of that lemon to juice. Not to mention the other lemons left on the counter to process.

Just because we made it through the juicer once doesn't mean we will never return. There is more juicing to be done.

We process this wide range of emotion and the stark realization that life has forever been changed while we are busy exploring the new territory of issues ahead. Parents often have little or no time to grieve and heal. We need to be functional almost immediately to meet the demands of our child. Life is full of sleepless nights, endless tears, fears, frustrations and medical appointments. The processing of emotions fits in around the busyness and often surfaces when we slow down to get much-needed rest.

There are no "super parents." It may be true that we develop great determination or superb coping skills, but if you were to ask, we would tell you that this journey is not what we wanted. The perception that I have it together is an illusion. I simply have to work harder, be more patient and give up more of myself on behalf of my child. This may not be fair, understood, valued or acknowledged, but it is the reality of my life.

Processing this range of emotions does not happen only once. Where death brings a degree of closure, those with disabled or ill children are faced every day with the source of their pain. We return to our grief from time to time simply because the source of the grief is still a tangible presence in our lives. Parents and caregivers of children with special needs will experience these emotional phases in varying degrees throughout the lives of their children.

A child's disability has a magnifying glass effect on the family. It often causes ordinary, everyday things – a temper tantrum, seeing another child, a worry, what someone else said – to become intensified, transformed and powerful. The issues of life seem larger because of the lemon.

Some parents compare their experience to riding an emotional roller coaster. Lori called it a loop. "You go through the stages of the process. I can be doing so well and then something just hits you and you are right back there at the bottom going through it again." Others call it chronic grief because it surfaces over and over.

I've also heard it described as a spiral. As the years go by, we keep coming back to the same intense emotions, issues and tasks. We struggle to maintain a balanced life, do too much work with not enough sleep, confront a health crisis, or celebrate some small accomplishment. But each time, we do so at a different level. Our child changes as he grows, and our journey changes us. So, how we face the tenth time around is different from how we rounded the second.

The intense sorrow and grief we felt when we first found out about our child's disability or disease is still a part of us. Like the emotions connected with other significant events in our lives, they may be exposed by unexpected words or events. We cannot choose these new moments of pain. We can neither anticipate nor avoid them.

Sometimes seeing typical kids achieving milestones reopens our grief.

I remember when Anna turned three and would start attending a regular preschool program instead of the sheltered toddler early intervention program. I went by myself to visit the new school, meet the staff and fill out the enrollment forms. While being given a tour of the classrooms, I saw other children a little older than Anna talking, playing and creating art projects far beyond any skills she had exhibited so far.

It felt like a slap in the face to realize how far behind she was developmentally. With all of the therapy at home and the intense school program, I had thought that we were making progress and catching up. It was a wake-up call to see how far we had to go, knowing how hard it had been to make the little progress we already had. The school director kindly let me sit on her couch and cry before we moved on to the forms.

I experienced the same shock when visiting the kindergarten classroom a few years later. The same surprise comes when I see Anna in a school program or at field days surrounded by her peers and see how small she is in comparison – or I find out what the rest of her class is working on academically and see the differences. I know Anna is behind her peers but it still hits me at moments. That hurts.

Another point of recurring grief comes when the behavior issues and quirks of autism or other conditions underscore how different our child is from their typical peers.

One of Noah's quirks has been temper tantrums that would last 30 to 45 minutes over minor events. He can have a difficult time processing everyday little things. He is learning to calm himself down within 10 or 12 minutes, realizing that what he is doing is not appropriate.

Shannon said that Noah also has an obsession with firemen and trains. He will walk up to anybody and start talking to them about his favorite subjects. People think, "That's odd."

Noah thrives on a routine. He has to sit at the same seat at the table. Nobody can take his seat at the table or it's a temper tantrum. The same thing happens over his place on the couch.

Another important routine for Noah is his bedtime rituals. Shannon has to say the same thing every night. They say their prayers and then she has to say the "Sweet dreams, don't let the bed bugs bite" saying – twice. Then Noah asks if the bathroom light is turned on. "Yes, Noah, it is." "Can I have a drink of water?" "Yes, you may." It is the same routine every night. Even if Noah is not at home, he has to call Shannon and she has to tell him the sweet dream saying.

While he is getting better about breaking out of his routines, Noah still needs a warning to avoid the temper tantrums. Noah also has to constantly reassure himself about time. "Do I go to school at 8:30?" "Do I go to swimming at 7:00 on Monday?"

When Lucas was younger, he was sometimes a runner – running away from Lori. He looked like a child who was misbehaving when he was having a meltdown or temper tantrum. Lori said, "It is amazing the things that people have said to me over the years about disciplining my child or making my child behave."

Lucas also had an obsession wanting people in the grocery store to have the little seat in their cart down. He would go through the store and, if somebody didn't have that little seat down, he would stick his hand through and put it down for them. Lori said, "After about the 4th time this poor man had gotten his seat knocked down by Lucas as we were going through the store, he lost it and said, 'What's the matter?' I was trying my best but there weren't two seats in a cart at that time. I couldn't put Lucas in the cart because he would fall over, plus I had the little one and groceries. I said, 'I'm sorry, he has autism, blah, blah, blah.' It turned out that his grandchild had just been diagnosed with autism shortly before that and I was able to hook him up with the Autism Society. Sometimes things work out in a weird way."

Another "Lucasism" was his obsession with different movies. As he learned to talk, instead of echoing one word back, he would memorize chunks of scenes from a movie – like a little recipe card file – and he would use that sentence in conversations. Once, during the Lion King era, he was in the grocery store and a woman said, "Oh, what a cute little boy. You're so sweet." And Lucas, in a big Scar character voice, said, "It's to die for." Lori wanted to melt into the floor. "Help me please get out of here," she thought. "You just never knew what was going to happen."

Lucas also paced in their backyard and escaped into, what Lori called, "Videoland." He did a finger waving self-stimulation motion while playing a movie in his mind. Lori thought that he inserted himself into the role of one of the characters. They try to keep him from doing this at inappropriate times but know that, when things are stressful at school, it is his way of calming himself down. He will escape into his own little world.

In addition to tuberous sclerosis, Kaylee has ADHD. She had a hard time focusing and used to act out a lot. She acted out in such a way that Jan had a hard time being friends with someone because Kaylee had such aggressive behaviors and was very unpredictable. It was a Jekyl and Hyde personality. Jan said, "Kaylee will slap me or hit me in the face or knock a hole in the wall and turn around and just be the most loving child. It's just messed up. It's a merry-go-round of emotions through little bits and pieces of the day."

Lisa described the "fingers of autism" like attention-deficit disorder, obsessive-compulsive disorder and food allergies that attach to autism and make each individual look and act different. Her son Spencer has more of the obsessive-compulsive disorder while Jess has more of the attention-deficit disorder.

Lisa called Wal-Mart "the biggest over-stimulant you can take an autistic child to. If you were to watch me, you would think this mother has no control over her disobedient children. Because, from the outside, it looks like they are normal and they are just very disobedient. But, of course, I know that's not true and that I do the best that I can. They can't communicate well and tend to act out."

For me, Anna has cycles of what I call the "giggling, limp noodle routine." Ever since she learned to walk, she will suddenly collapse as though her legs won't support her weight any longer. I am left holding her upright by her hand. She picks the ideal locations for such behavior – crossing the street or parking lot, stores, walking among a crowd at a football game, whenever I am carrying loads of stuff or holding her younger brother. It is hilarious to her and she will giggle, say "Anna is a very bad girl" and giggle some more. Meanwhile, I try to ignore her (confrontations only make it worse, especially in public) and end up dragging her to where we are going.

At times, Anna is also a runner. She will slip her tiny hand out of mine, like Houdini, and take off running, primarily in crowded parking lots and along busy streets or wherever there is an audience to see me fall apart in frustration. She won't come when I call her and sometimes the best solution is to ignore her until she comes back. Other times, safety demands that I give chase.

Anna also becomes obsessed with a certain object and searches for it everywhere she goes. The latest have included fire hydrants, train crossing signals, electrical outlets, light switches, stop signs and the word "must" on road signs (like "Right lane must turn right.")

When Anna was a toddler, her brother Luke was just 15 months behind her in age but ahead of her developmentally. In teaching the rules and consequences, we had to enforce them consistently for Luke's sake but I wondered if Anna even understood the rules. Other times, I wondered if her behaviors were part of her disability or just plain old disobedience. I wished for a light on her forehead, like the lights on the dashboard of my car, to give me an indication if she understood.

Difficulty learning typical life skills also highlights differences. Lisa was in the middle of trying to potty train Spencer but he simply didn't understand the concept of getting it into the toilet. So, he had many, many accidents. It's one thing to carry diapers around for your infant but not for a 5-year-old who just doesn't get it. Lisa wanted to go out and do things but Spencer's issues made it very difficult.

One day, Spencer messed his pants and Lisa just lost it. "I can't do this anymore," she said. "I picked him up by his arms and helped him up the stairs so he wouldn't get everything everywhere and set him on the toilet. And, he just stared at me with a blank face, not getting it. And I sat down on the floor in the bathroom and just bawled my head off. I couldn't deal with it anymore. I actually started yelling about it saying, 'I can't do this anymore! I can't do this.' When I started saying that, I realized that I'm not supposed to do this."

Shannon remembered a time their family was at the Wild Animal Park. Their family hadn't taken Noah to big parks before because of the over-stimulation factor but decided to try when he was about 5. "Noah was spitting and pulling his shirt off as we were standing in line," said Shannon. "He was on the floor, grunting and pulling his hair out and everyone was just looking at us. I was thinking that we were never doing this again. It was not worth it."

Later, a friend told Shannon and Ray about special assistance passes at Disney parks. Shannon had grown up going to Disney so they got the pass and didn't have to wait in any lines. They had the best time. From the outside, things look normal with Noah but there are definite issues. As Shannon said, "We can't go if we have to wait in line. It's not fun for any of us – so why go? That is nice that Disney does that for families."

Sometimes the issues are sensory. Lucas has food issues and cannot handle certain textures. He wears headphones when his family goes to church to block out the loud sound of the worship band. All of his senses are hypersensitive. Smells that don't normally bother the general population, really set him off. He talks about seeing the "fuzzies in the air" (dust) when it's not necessarily in the sunlight. He also can't touch newspapers and gets freaked out if he has to touch one for a school report. Plus, his logic, gait and intonation are not quite where they should be.

Lucas also had an issue called mind-blindness. He assumed that his parents knew the things he was thinking just because he was thinking them. One time, while still living in Wisconsin, he was supposed to ride the bus home from school the day before Christmas break. When he didn't get off the bus, Lori called the school and someone went outside looking for him. He was standing outside, on a zero-degree day, waiting for Lori to come pick him up like she had on the last day before Christmas break the year before. In his mind, the pattern was set and he assumed that Lori knew he would be waiting to get picked up.

We may be prepared for life's big battles but it is the daily skirmishes, failures and frustrations that rob us of our inner calm. Lori said, "I could handle the big problems that came up but it was the little ones that drove me crazy. Like, I just wanted to get Lucas' hair cut without a meltdown. We got kicked out of more places. I would cut his hair in the bathtub or sneak in at night when he was sleeping. He had the worst haircut for years when he was younger. It just seems so silly now when I think back, but those were the kind of things that I struggled with."

Fresh pain also comes when our child is subjected to rejection or bullying by their peers or when we face the criticism and comments of other adults. Appearing in public with a wheelchair user opens us up to unwelcome stares and thoughtless comments from curious children and adults who should know better. For hidden disabilities, nothing stings more that the unwanted attention of strangers loudly misjudging our child.

For Shannon, little bouts of sadness come when she thinks of Noah's future and his not having peers his own age that want to play with him. For example, if they schedule a play date for

Noah, children come over and play with his brother Casey instead. Noah wants to have a play date because his brother has them, but when the day comes, he plays with the others as long as the activity is one he wants to do. Otherwise, he is fine being on his own and doesn't mingle with the others. The hardest part for Shannon is when Casey gets invited somewhere with a friend and Noah is left behind.

Lori remembered kids purposely trying to get a rise out of Lucas because he would do something weird. "I remember his lunchbox being hidden behind the toilet." She also remembered a day when his class had been on a trip and was having their group picture taken on the steps. "We got the picture back and he wasn't in the picture. He cried because he wasn't in the group. I said, 'Where did you want to be?' Lucas said, 'I wanted to be in the middle.' Those feelings are there even if the experts say kids with autism don't have or need friends."

When Anna was in kindergarten, I would wait with her outside the school every morning until the bell rang for her to go inside. One day, I noticed a group of boys from her class, standing around her laughing. Anna was smiling but I stepped closer to eavesdrop. The boys would say, "Anna, say poop" and Anna would say "poop." They thought it was hilarious because she would say whatever they wanted her to say. She thought they liked her and that it was a fun game. My heart broke but I was grateful she didn't understand their teasing.

On the other hand, David struggled with peers and fully understood their rejection. He was with the same group of children year after year in elementary school, and by 5th grade, the growing animosity towards him was vicious.

During gym class, the children would play baseball and David was forced to be on one of the teams. Every day he was the last one to be picked. The kids didn't understand that if there was an odd number, the team that picked first would get David. So, David would be standing alone while everybody on both teams would be arguing and screaming, "We don't want him on our team."

Once he was forced to be on one of the teams, his teammates

were really angry at him. He couldn't come close to hitting a ball because of his eye-hand coordination problems. He couldn't get within a foot of the ball and it was humiliating. On the way home from school, other kids would throw rocks or snowballs at him, taunt him, shove him down and call him names. Sherilyn said, "I think that kind of treatment does more damage to the soul than the fact that you can't run as fast as somebody else or you can't hit a baseball."

In the meantime, Sherilyn and her new husband Steve had two babies a year apart. David was dealing with the hatred at school and seeing a psychologist for help while suddenly losing the undivided attention of his parents at home. It was a horrible time in his life and it wasn't fun for Sherilyn either.

My fears about Anna's safety and doing whatever somebody told her to do hit home on a summer afternoon. Anna (1st grade) and her brother Luke (kindergarten) were playing in the neighborhood with a couple of other boys.

From inside our house, I heard a blood-curdling scream and loud crying that I recognized as Anna's. I rushed outside to see Anna running across the street with blood streaming down her face and leaving a trail up the driveway. Who thinks about white carpet at a time like this? I'm ashamed to say – me. I made her lay down on our front porch and then ran inside to get a couple of towels and a wet washcloth. Back outside, I wiped at the blood on her face and tried to find where it was coming from, while a pool of blood formed under her head.

Of course, my husband arrived home in the middle of the chaos. I finally found the injury on the top of Anna's head and got the bleeding slowed and the blood sopped up. I carried Anna inside, held her head over the edge of the bathtub and poured pitchers of water over her hair until it ran light pink. There was a gash on the top of her head that required staples at the emergency room (and a mandatory reporting by the hospital staff that led to a visit by a police officer to our home).

Meanwhile, Luke came home and we started to piece together the story. We learned the oldest boy had told Anna to go down in a window-well and go to the bathroom down there, saying she couldn't come out until she did. He told the youngest boy to hit Anna with a golf club if she tried to get out or else he wouldn't play with him ever again. The youngest boy had gone running home after the incident and had also appeared on our porch with his stepfather. His face was sheet-white when he saw all of the blood. He later brought over a stuffed animal and card for Anna (that he had to pay for with extra chores at home) and apologized over and over for hitting Anna. No apology ever came from the other boy involved.

Other painful moments come through the comments of others. Doctors and even friends urged Gene and Ruth Ann to put Johnny into an institution because it would be "easier on the family." "The baby will become such a burden to your girls," said a friend. "He will never sit, walk, or talk. I'm certain that you and Ruth Ann just aren't up to the demands that go along with raising this kind of child," said one of the doctors. "He'll hinder your chances of becoming a successful coach," said another friend.[xix]

Gene said, "One of the reasons I felt that people kept urging us to institutionalize Johnny was that there was a certain embarrassment among some folks when they had to confront a 'retarded' child." [xx]

A new educational challenge or diagnosis can also set us back emotionally.

After years of instruction at her level, Anna was actually reading. In fact, in the 4th grade, she was decoding or sounding out words at a 2nd grade level. However, she could not retell the story or answer oral questions about what she had just read. On the other hand, given written multiple-choice questions, she had perfect comprehension.

Something unusual was going on but it was a mystery to most of her educational team. Then, a new speech therapist joined the staff and she brought the answer – hyperlexia.

Hyperlexia is a precocious ability with words, often found with autism and evidenced by a gap between decoding ability and comprehension. Looking back, Anna never drew pictures. She instead wrote letter after letter and word after word, filling pages with writing.

The same thing was happening in her brain. When reading, she held onto the letters and didn't create a mental picture. For example, if she read, "The lady had a red hat," she visualized the letters that made up each word. She did not imagine a woman carrying or wearing a red hat. Therefore, when asked questions, she had to sort through the letters instead of referring to her mental image.

It was heartbreaking, as a mother, avid reader and writer, to realize my daughter could not understand anything I wrote. I thought, "What's the point of being able to read if you don't understand the meaning?"

At other times, a new health challenge puts us back on the juicer, wringing out new emotions.

When Anna was three years old, she started to periodically injure herself. Without notice, she would throw herself onto the floor or against walls, banging her head. She would scratch and tear at her face. She yanked chunks of her hair out. She would bite the back of her hand and rip it away. Screaming and arching her back, she was out of control.

Confused as to the trigger for these bizarre and self-destructive behaviors, I asked friends from the CdLS online support group for advice. Unanimously, they replied to have her checked for acid reflux. Children with CdLS often self-injure to distract themselves from the pain of gastro-esophageal reflux disease (GERD).

When chewing an antacid tablet would quickly transform her back into our darling little girl, we knew we had found the answer. Tests and prescription medications resolved most of her issues. But, while we waited for her hair to re-grow and her skin to heal, I remembered the agony of seeing her out of control, hurting herself, and not knowing how to help her.

Jan finally worked through her anger and depression and was able to put the pieces of her life back together with God's help. Then, Kaylee was diagnosed with a brain tumor. One of the tubors in her brain had developed into a giant cell astrocytoma in a horrible location. The tumor type was very unpredictable and it was uncertain whether doctors would be able to operate or not based on its location. "I don't know if she is going to live or die. Can somebody tell me that?" said Jan. "Is our suffering not enough that we have to add this?" The family could only wait to see if the tumor grew and if Kaylee developed other symptoms.

Adam made it through the initial phases of chemotherapy. His family was looking forward to the maintenance phase of his treatment where he would begin to take milder doses.

On the first day of the maintenance phase, on his 16th birthday, Adam had several mini-strokes. The blood vessels in his brain were collapsing. They spent the evening in the emergency room at Children's Hospital where Adam slept curled up in an infant crib because it was the only room available that night.

A year and a half later, just before his senior year of high school, Adam dove into a lake and scraped his face on the bottom. Sherilyn said, "He was just a mess of blood and raw skin. When I saw him, he had blood dripping from his face." Adam already had pink eye and they were monitoring his temperature daily because his immune system would shut down with the chemo. They picked up medication on their way out of town for a scheduled vacation.

By the last day of vacation, Adam's face had scabbed over but his pink eye wasn't getting any better. Sherilyn said, "He was starting to drag and complaining of a headache and being a little nauseated. We got home and he barely made it to the bathroom to throw up. I kept taking his temperature. He had a temperature but it wasn't high." Her calls to Children's Hospital didn't provide the answers since the oncology clinic was closed.

Every time Sherilyn would ask Adam how he was doing, he would say, "Fine" but not mention the fact that he was throwing up every day. He wasn't a complainer but he was very sick. One night, he came downstairs angry because he had been upstairs throwing up and now his stomach was in such extreme pain, he was about to pass out. Sherilyn grabbed some clothes and rushed him to the emergency room at Children's Hospital while her husband Steve made phone calls ahead of them.

When they arrived, they learned that Adam's pancreas had shut down. His immune system was at an extreme low and his pink eye was off the charts. Adam was in such intense pain, he was immediately admitted to the oncology ward where they began pumping his stomach. His whole digestive system had shut down and he was beginning to bloat.

Adam was taken off the chemotherapy in hopes that his immune system could start to rebuild. After four days of pumping his stomach, the doctors realized that Adam must have some sort of blockage in his intestines. "We've got to go in and do exploratory surgery and take care of this problem," they told Sherilyn.

Sherilyn, at a low because of little sleep for four days, worried aloud. "You want to go in and do invasive, infectious surgery on Adam. If he can't even get over pink eye, how is his body going to heal? How is he going to recover and fight any infection? There's nothing in his immune system responses that says he can survive a surgery."

The doctor just looked at Sherilyn and said, "I can not tell you he is going to live through this, but we cannot let him continue in this kind of intense pain. We have to at least try to fix it."

After Adam was prepped for surgery, there was a delay. Finally, another doctor came out and said, "The doctor who was supposed to perform this surgery has been held up by another surgery. I'm going to be handling Adam's case now. Before we do something as invasive as this, I would like to make three one-inch incisions and use a small camera to look around and see if we can find the problem area. If we find it, we can go in and take care of it. Otherwise, we're going to close him back up, continue to pump his stomach and hope that his pancreas will start working the longer he is off the chemo."

Sherilyn agreed with the new focus and nothing was found with the camera. Therefore, the staff continued to pump Adam's stomach for another 4 or 5 days while people across the country were praying for his recovery. Adam's pain began to lessen and finally he was able to pass a bubble of gas through his digestive system. Things really started moving the next couple of days and soon Adam was out of bed and trying to walk again.

Thom's unique cancer responded to the chemotherapy. By Christmas, his stomach was completely back to normal size. Other than the chemo routine in the hospital, his life returned to normal activities.

Then, early in the year, Linda found a woman with three children wandering in the clinic. The children obviously had chicken pox, a dreaded disease for cancer patients. While the family was quickly escorted off the floor, they had time to leave the deadly virus in the air. Sure enough, in a few weeks, several children came down with the chicken pox. That meant they could not continue their chemo until completely well again.

Thom's sister and brother came down with the chicken pox too and Linda made a quick call to the hospital. Vaccine from the Atlanta Center was quickly flown out for Thom. Linda and Keith picked it up at the airport and delivered it directly to the hospital. Linda said, "Thom still got the chicken pox but they were of a different variety. They came in 50 spots the size of a dime."

Before long, the effect of the chicken pox began to emerge. Thom's cancer got a foothold back and soon his lungs filled with fluid. He was placed back in the hospital where the liquid was drained. Thom began his chemo again, but this time the results were not as dramatic.

In the spring of that year, Thom's doctors told Linda and Keith that things were not going well. They hoped to put Thom on an older routine of drugs in order to get the cancer back into remission. The recommended drug could cause permanent kidney damage unless it was flushed out of the system as quickly as possible. Linda said, "We worked to get Thom's urine output up but much of the liquid he took stayed in his tummy area again giving him a huge stomach and waistline." Another month or so later and it was apparent that this chemotherapy routine could no longer be used on Thom because he could not flush enough of the liquid out his system.

Their next setback came when they were told there was nothing more that could be done for Thom. After hearing the news, Linda went back to Thom's room sad and tearful. Linda said, "Thom asked what was wrong and I said that I had received some bad news. He said if it was what he thought, it was good news for him because he would not have to have another awful bone marrow test. What an attitude. He knew that death was only the last step of this journey on earth but the first step of the new journey in the next."

Of their options, Linda immediately told the doctor they wanted to take Thom home. "In order for us to do this, I was taught to give him his pain shots every four hours. Believe me, it is easier to give shots to the practice orange than to the patient," said Linda. "When I passed the test, Thom was packed up and we carried him home. The last week of his life was special."

Thom spent many hours listening to his favorite song, "Going Home." Although the shots were to be given every four hours, they did not cover the pain for the full four hours. Linda said, "We spent that last half hour reading Raggedy Ann and Andy and Winnie the Pooh stories while lying in hot water in the tub." Thom could not keep food down but still enjoyed eating. So, he ate and then threw up his dinner. His last meal was McDonald's French fries and a Coke, requested with a gurgle in his voice because he was filling with fluid. He stopped breathing on Friday afternoon.

The recurring grief due to Thom's battle with cancer found a sense of closure. About the time Thom passed away, Linda found a book about the stages of grief. "This helped me as I learned to continue life. I had not been prepared for the hole left in my everyday life when Thom's life ended."

After the emotional turmoil of shock, grief, denial, anger, guilt, blame, and depression, we eventually reach what experts call acceptance. We regain our equilibrium and sense of well being and begin to function as we had before the crisis or trauma.

Human nature dictates that we will change whatever we can and worry about those things we cannot. Accepting unpleasant truths is not something that comes easily to most of us. Yet for parents raising special needs children, achieving some degree of acceptance is vital. Acceptance is when we are able to view the event and its effects within the greater context of life.

Moving towards acceptance means letting go of emotional connections to the past, letting go of hopes and expectations and acknowledging things as they truly are – not how I wish they could be. While I acknowledge the difficulties of my situation, I also see the good things that exist in my life and find the strength and willingness to seek them out.

I have to accept the fact that until my children are grown and stable, my life will constantly be in motion. My children will always have needs, and at the drop of a hat, I will need to put down what I was doing and go help.

We work through the initial shock and emotions by the busyness and business of responding to the specific issues our child's disability or disease involves. Our family reorganizes itself around the reality of our new circumstances and we adapt to our new roles.

We may eventually arrive at acceptance, but there will still be quick trips back to the other emotions.

Processing emotions is not fun or easy, but it is as necessary as juicing lemons is to making lemonade. Do you feel like you are on the juicer of life? Your feelings are real and normal. Acknowledge the process and get through the emotions. However long that takes is as individual as we are.

I am reminded of Jesus' disciples standing at the tomb. They felt lost, afraid, confused and abandoned. It was Friday, but Sunday was coming.

With all of our sour, painful feelings, there is still hope. It's time to add the sugar. Because, through God's strength, we can face the future.

In Your Kitchen

We must allow ourselves to grieve our losses. Here is one tool to help.

1) Give the loss a name. Identify it and learn about it.

2) Feel the pain involved with the loss and identify what you are feeling. Don't try to change your feelings.

3) Express your feelings to others who are supportive. Join a support group, find someone you can call anytime, seek professional counseling, or find someone to pray with.

4) Allow yourself to grieve to completion. Don't try to short-circuit the process. Give yourself permission to take as much time as you need to work through your loss.

5) Write a letter to God telling Him how you really feel about your lemon situation(s).

5 - ADDING SUGAR

Sherilyn, in Colorado, received a phone call from North Platte, Nebraska. The doctor on the other end of the line delivered the blow that Adam, her 15-year-old son, had no platelets in his blood, had leukemia and might not survive the trip to Children's Hospital in Denver.

After hanging up the phone, Sherilyn sank into a chair, terrified that she was going to lose her son. She put her head down and began to pray. "God, I need a word picture. I need to know that You are here right now. I need to know that You at least know what's going on with Adam in Nebraska."

Sherilyn thought the answer to her prayer might be a picture of Jesus sitting on the desk next to her. Or of Jesus sitting on Adam's hospital bed. Instead, she saw a vivid image from her past.

Raised in a very dysfunctional family, there came a day when Sherilyn was 17 that her mother picked up a knife off the kitchen counter. She yanked Sherilyn up against her front and held the knife to Sherilyn's throat and threatened to slit it. "I could feel her shaking from rage and the knife vibrating against my throat," said Sherilyn.

Years later, Sherilyn asked Jesus, "Were you there when my mom held the knife to my throat?" In answer, she said, "I could see Jesus standing there facing us while my mom and I were having this heated argument. The second my mom picked up the knife and wrapped her arms around me, I looked down and saw Jesus' arms. He was behind my mom and had His arms wrapped around my mom. And, as I looked down, I saw that His hand was holding my mom's hand that was holding the knife."

"I realized in that moment," said Sherilyn, "that God loved my mom and He loved me. He protected both of us that day. All my fear and everything inside just melted and turned to joy. No one, including my mom, could hurt me because Jesus was holding the hand that was holding the knife. Unless it was God's desire to let that happen, it wasn't going to happen. It didn't happen because God was in control and had a different plan."

So, when Adam was diagnosed with leukemia, Sherilyn asked God for a word picture. Instantly, she saw Jesus holding her mother's hand that was holding the knife. She never expected that answer to her prayer but was flooded with an overwhelming, unexplainable, incomprehensible peace. "It didn't mean that Adam was going to live or that he was going to die. It simply meant that Jesus was in control and I could experience peace even when I didn't know the outcome."

After having her husband Steve pulled off the golf course, she told him about the doctor's phone call and they prayed together. Sherilyn also told Steve about the word picture and both were enveloped in peace. As Sherilyn said, "When you can face the possible death of your child in peace, you can have the most incredible adventure."

When faced with darkest night – we need light. When tossed and turned by storms – we need a safe harbor. When making lemonade from sour events – we need the sugar of hope.

Paul wrote, "We are hard pressed on every side, but not crushed; perplexed, but not in despair; persecuted, but not abandoned; struck down, but not destroyed."[xxi] Some days our burdens seem too heavy. Things happen and we feel crushed, abandoned or in despair. How is it possible to not feel this way? These early Christians were hard pressed by the circumstances, but their hearts were not crushed. In the middle of the darkest circumstances, their hearts were lifted by hope.

Our despair is heavy and pulls us down. Hope lifts and bubbles up inside. Hope does not depend on the circumstances because real hope has very little to do with what is going on around us. We hold this hope: Christ died for us, therefore we can live.

We need hope in the middle of life's challenges. The optimism carries us over the rough spots because our new perspective sees beyond our circumstances. Hope helps us through life's experiences with humor and compassion, accepts reality, reflects without regret and strives for what can be.

Hope brings the excitement of tomorrow. It involves putting our faith into action when it would be easier to doubt. It believes that God has made a promise to take care of us. Hope anticipates this will happen. Hope opens its hands to what a loving Father sends.

Wishing is not the same thing as hoping. Wishing has no reality base. Instead, it indulges in fantasy. Hope, on the other hand, contains a realistic expectation of being fulfilled.

Life is fragile and our days are full of uncertainties. Yet, regardless of what happens today, or tomorrow, or next year, hope is alive. We willingly set our troubles and doubts aside in favor of the belief that God can solve the problem or that there is a greater good to come from this situation.

Barbara Gill wrote the following about hope but I think something vital is missing. Can you find it? "God forbid anyone should go around entertaining false hopes! But in a certain sense, what other kind of hope is there? Hope is the thing that is willing to take a chance on the future. And who is audacious enough to say what the future will bring? Hope is the capacity to see something on the horizon that we are willing to move toward. If our hope gets us from today to tomorrow, and in that new day we are ready or able to deal with something we thought we couldn't face, then hope has done its job. There is a worse thing than false hope. It is no hope."xxii

Another traveler on the journey of life wrote from a different perspective. "Hope has no strength of its own. We can't hope in hope; we have to put our hope in something else. So the strength of hope lies in what it hopes in. That means that what we put our hope in really matters. If we put our hope in lesser things, we set ourselves up for disappointment. If we hope that we'll get a promotion and our boss favors someone else, we're crushed. But if we put our hope in God's provision for our lives, promotion or not, our hope grows as we see God work, because we've put our hope in something strong enough to sustain us."xxiii

This second hope is built on faith. Hebrews 11:1 says, "Now faith is being sure of what we hope for and certain of what we do not see." The rest of the chapter lists those whose hope in God carried them though the trials of life.

God is the author, foundation and source of true hope. True hope says that God is in control. True hope says this difficulty is temporary. True hope says that we are not alone. True hope says that God will help me along the way. Let's look deeper at these messages of hope.

God is God and I am not. He is the one in control and not me. God isn't nervous because I don't like what I'm going through. The mystery of the situation is in His hands. I don't know everything and He demands that I trust Him, even when I don't understand. Isaiah wrote, "As the heavens are higher than the earth, so are [God's] ways higher than your ways and [God's] thoughts than your thoughts."xxiv

Within days of learning Anna had Cornelia de Lange syndrome, friends gave us a plaque that still hangs on our wall. It reads: "Sometimes God calms the storm . . . And sometimes He lets the storm rage and calms His child." I may not understand why He calms one and not the other, but God is in control and it is His decision to make.

Our search for real hope leads us to the only source that can truly satisfy. When I'm feeling lost and out of control, I hope desperately that someone else is in control. I long to know that there is order beyond the universe and that things make sense somewhere no matter how messed up they seem down here. But only God can bring that level of assurance, because He is the One in control. And as I discover that God is looking after me, I am able to put more and more of my trust in Him.

A clear example of my lack of control rests with the not-so-simple beating of my heart. The intricate timing or sinus rhythm has nothing to do with me, my will, or my plans. I have no power over my own heartbeat. Only God controls that. My heart and my life are in His hands and so is my complete confidence.

When faced with health situations, it helps to remember that we can't even change the beat of our own hearts. God can. We don't know what will happen to us physically. God does. We can do nothing more than trust Him because the womb-weaver is also the life-sustainer.

Matthew 17:20 tells us, "If you have faith as small as a mustard seed, you can say to this mountain, 'Move from here to there,' and it will move. Nothing will be impossible for you." How often do we pray in faith asking God to move the mountain? God is more than able to do a miracle if He chooses to.

Faith trusts Him when the miracle doesn't happen the way I thought. Sometimes miracles are hidden or look different than what we ordered. Perhaps the true miracle is when hope and faith surround us in the middle of tears and disappointment. The miracle is when my human heart accepts God's sovereignty.

Shannon claimed the verse, "With man this is impossible, but with God all things are possible."[xxv] "That's what we claim for Noah's healing. God can heal autism. If He does in this lifetime, He does. If not, that's His timing. We just have to put our faith in Him."

Can medicine scientifically factor the impact our love, faith, and prayers will have on our children's future? Of course not. So, then, it stands to reason that any medical prognosis is only a guess.

For some, it helps to rely on the promise in Jeremiah 29:11 – "For I know the plans I have for you,' declares the Lord, 'plans to prosper you and not to harm you, plans to give you hope and a future." My child has a future. One that is designed by the hand of the Almighty Creator. For today, it's okay that I don't know what the future holds. It's enough just knowing who holds the future.

Remember, the character of the One in charge does not change. Another plaque on my wall reminds me that "Life is hard but God is good." He is always good and I can trust Him to make the best decisions, even if I don't understand them.

Hope says this is temporary. We know we can face anything with courage and peace when we immerse ourselves in the hope of God's promises for our eternal future. Because of the hope Jesus shared with us, we can wait, even in places of fear and darkness, with courage and fortitude. We know that, whatever the immediate outcome, our long-term future is secured.

We pray for rescue from our situation. We pray that suffering will be eased, that challenges will be overcome, that lives will be spared. Yet we know that even if God's answer is not the answer that we asked for, everything will be all right in the end. Hope holds us securely through the difficulties of this life until we reach our heavenly home.

We can endure this season, because it is temporary and will pass on. Even if the season lasts this entire blip of an earthly lifetime. Jan said, "If the unthinkable happens, there is the next chapter of life. God knows what is next. Kaylee won't have illness in heaven and I will see her there. We will still recognize each other. Knowing and believing in the hereafter helps."

Roxanne said their faith was important when talking to other parents who had lost a child. "They didn't have a belief system," she said, "and were hoping that their child was in heaven but they didn't know. We knew for sure where Sunni Anne was – right in the arms of Jesus."

We can live as though we know everything is going to be okay. Because we do! God promised to use everything that happens in our lives for our good. On the other side of our trials, heaven awaits.

As someone said, "Everything will be okay in the end. If it's not okay, it's not the end!"

Not only is God in control, He loves me. He loved me so much He sent His Son to take my rightful punishment on the cross. He adopted me into His family. He forgives, protects, comforts and provides for me. He is preparing a place for me. Because of His great love, He is with me and I am not alone.

"When faced with difficulties as a parent," Sherilyn said, "you learn to stand alone. The wife may learn to do what needs to be done at home while her husband is away at work (or vice versa). Friends will come alongside you in the beginning, but they can't walk that path with you every single day. You can't expect them to. And you are going to have to journey this alone, as far as other people are concerned, and there will be times that you feel you are all alone. When you trust that God is with you, you are never alone."

Even when things seem hopeless, God is there beside me to guide and protect me. He can turn my darkest hours into blessings of peace, love and closeness to Him. I'm reminded of the familiar "Footprints" poem when, during the difficult times, there was only one set of footprints in the sand. In the poem, God said those were the times He was carrying the author. Through it all, God is with me and never lets go of me. That's one reason "They will call him Immanuel – which means, 'God with us.'"[xxvi]

The weather turned bad with lightning and Adam couldn't be

transported to Children's Hospital by Flight for Life. Sherilyn was able to talk to him and Adam was scared to death. Sherilyn told him, "You need to get real with God and tell Him that you need to know that He is with you. Tell Him you need to feel His presence. Tell Him you are ready to get real with Him and ask Him to be real with you." She said that Adam then prayed during the whole ambulance ride to Denver.

During the first week in the hospital, Adam was pumped full of platelets and medications to help him get over the yellow jaundice so he could then start chemotherapy. Doctors put a port in his heart and did a lot of tests. Finally, after over a week, they were on their way home. Adam turned to his mother. "Hasn't this been an amazing week?"

Sherilyn was busy driving on the interstate highway. "Uh. What are you talking about? Did I miss something or did you just get diagnosed with cancer?"

"Mom," Adam replied, "I did just what you told me to do. I got real with God. I never knew you could feel the presence of God. All the way to the hospital, I just talked to God and I told Him, 'I'm not asking You to heal me or anything like that, but if You'll just let them know what it is. I know You'll be with me and help me and I promise, with Your help, I will do anything they ask me to do and be a good sport about it. Just tell them what to do to get me through this." He memorized Philippians 4:13 (NKJV), "I can do all things through Christ who strengthens me." Adam said, "Through everything they did to me with the tests and the port surgery, I felt God's presence. Every moment I was in the hospital. Isn't that cool to know that there is a God and you can really feel His presence?"

Of course, Sherilyn had to pull off the highway. She was crying and shaking and so excited. The night before sending Adam away to camp, she and Steve had prayed that God would get a hold of Adam's heart. While they certainly didn't expect it through cancer, God answered that prayer.

Like the promise Adam memorized and eventually had tattooed on his arm, we know that God strengthens us. He also leads and guides us, brings people across our path to help and gives us wisdom when we need it most. Each day of caring for our special children is a step of faith. We are on a journey, watching to see how God will meet our every need. He will prove His faithfulness over and over again along the way. When there is not the miraculous cure we prayed for, He will comfort us, strengthen us and help us cope with our day-to-day struggles.

Linda said, "Our walk with God continued on course but there was a different kind of confidence. God had trusted us with a huge problem and with His help, we had succeeded in that situation. God received the glory and we were able to bear witness to His strength in every situation."

It's only through God's grace that I don't shrink back from life's challenges. I'm continually amazed that when I trust God enough to take a step toward Him in hope, faith, or courage, He meets me right there. And then equips me to take the next step. I've found this to be true over and over in my journey.

Sometimes we find the right doctor at just the right time. God led Shannon and Ray to the PROMPT program in New Mexico and later to a trained therapist in their area. Roxanne and Tony have seen God bring the right person at the right time every step along the way. They have even told doctors and teachers, "We feel like you are the person that God wants on the case right now and it's up to you whether you want to take that on." It was clear to them that the expertise of the professionals had come along just for Rob.

For us, I had to quickly (and randomly) pick a pediatrician from the insurance company list. Before I was rolled into the operating room for the c-section delivery, we met our choice for the first time. It turns out, he was a fellow believer and prayed with us right there. Several years later, God used a woman in our church to hand us the information about treating brain injuries that radically changed Anna's development.

God can also put us in the right location. Lisa said, "It's a miracle that we live where we do. We moved to Fort Collins just because we wanted to, and yet Fort Collins has been in the top-ten in the nation for autism research, development and help in the school system. It's a miracle that we are in an area where we can get help in a school district. Otherwise, I would have to pay for tutors and find help from other places. God guided us to the area He knew that we needed to be in order to get the help that we needed. That has been huge."

Other times, God brings along encouragement when we need it most. Lisa was feeling pretty low after reading an article in Time magazine about autism. She stayed up late that night because she was so upset. The next day at church, the pastor said some things in his sermon that triggered the deep sorrow she was feeling. "I thought that I needed to talk to him. So, after the service, I walked up and talked to him. He said, 'You know, I was flying home last night on an airplane and I picked up a copy of Time magazine. I read this article about autism and I prayed for Spencer.' That little bit showed me that there was hope and it turned my thinking from sorrow to hope. That God would talk to somebody else and have them pray for my son. That gave me a glimpse of hope."

God also supplies wisdom. Shannon and Ray pray before going into IEP (Individualized Education Plan) meetings. We prayed for wisdom to discover why Anna was self-injuring. We have prayed for help finding her glasses including in the irrigation ditch, over the back fence and even after she flushed the $300 titanium frames down the toilet.

Some days our miracle answer is simply having the strength and courage to face another day. Roxanne said, "We've just always known that God would get us through whatever the issue was or the hurdle. It's been a hurdle every step along the way." Lisa often tries to handle things with her first-born go-getter attitude. "God is there for me and waiting every time I jump into the wagon acting like I can do this alone. Every time I have my breakdown, He gently reminds me that I'm not supposed to carry it all."

There is a popular saying to the effect that God never gives us more than we can handle. Others say this in an attempt to comfort. They are trying to say the right thing and be helpful but it is not always received that way. Some who hear this statement don't feel comforted to hear they have been handpicked for a task that feels unfair and overwhelming. They did not feel at all qualified or capable of carrying the load.

I remember hearing "special children for special parents." Well, for once in my life, I wanted to be ordinary. I didn't want to be special. Would I have chosen this? But then, I didn't get to choose.

When faced with such an enormous task, we sometimes wonder why God would let this happen to us. And if we don't feel equipped to handle it, we might wonder if this is a punishment or God's testing to see if we will pass or fail.

Jan, at first, did not like either the saying or the people who said it to her. She has since realized their good intentions and says a simple "Thank you" in return. "My friend was repeating that one and she said, 'They say God doesn't give you more than you can handle. Well, He just did!' I love the honesty of that response," said Jan.

A few hours after learning Anna's diagnosis, I recalled this familiar saying. My reaction was a little different. I thought, "If God doesn't give me more than I can handle, then He must know me better than I know myself, because I don't think I can do this." I have later grown to realize that God *does* allow more than we can handle . . . alone. He can handle it and, with His help, so can I.

I have come to recognize that God is very purposeful in what He does. The fact He would grant me a special child or a special burden means that He will also equip me to carry it. It makes me wonder if perhaps God is trusting me.

Lisa said, "It's not that God gives us what we can't handle, although it might seem like He does. But He doesn't. And, if it's an overwhelming situation, He does give us help. He gives us tools. He gives us the means if we are just obedient to Him and listen."

So, how do we move from the sour emotions of anger, guilt, blame, despair and depression toward the sugar of hope? One step at a time. It starts by being honest with God about what you are feeling and even asking Him the tough questions. The Psalmist asked God "Why?" and "How long?" many times. He set an example of pouring out his troubles to God in an honest dialogue.

We can be honest with God. Tell Him exactly how you feel. Share your disappointments, fears, and anger. Reveal any self-blame you are hiding in your heart. Give all of your guilt over to God. Just don't, in the middle of pain, throw away God because He is the key to blessing and the source of hope.

I've gone through seasons of asking "Why?" though I've never asked "Why me?" It's only through God's grace that my attitude has been more of "Why not me?" Suffering exists on this earth and it can happen to anyone. Why cancer? Why stillborn babies? Why cancer? Why grace? Why love? Why forgiveness? Maybe "Why" is not a useful question. Maybe the real question is "What now?"

It's okay to be mad at God and question Him. Just keep the conversation going and eventually His love and hope will trickle through to your shattered soul. Just a spark of hope can cause us to start to listen. As that hope grows, like the tiny mustard seed of faith, it can move mountains. Eventually, we arrive at conclusions about God and find peace and hope . . . for this crisis. With the next round of lemons, we can forget or lose our focus. We then need fresh hope. Maybe that's why Jeremiah said that God's mercies were fresh every morning because we need a new batch every day![xxvii]

In case you think you need to work hard to find God, consider the 14th century German theologin Meister Eckhart who believed that "God is like a person who clears his throat while hiding and so gives himself away."

One of Anna's favorite games is hide-and-seek but she's always easy to find because she always gives herself away. I might be searching in the bathroom or a closet and, from another part of the room, I'll hear her giggle. As though I am so close, she couldn't stand for me not to find her.

As if a giggle wasn't enough of a clue, she will say, "I'm in Anna's room" or "I'm under my bed." She invariably is either in her favorite hiding place or in the place I was hiding in my last turn. Her hiding places remind me that God is right where I was hiding and He even says, "Here I am."

Other parents have made this journey from questioning to hope. After the baby Roxanne and Tony were trying to adopt died, their pastor said, "I'm so glad that I'm not in a situation where I have to talk to people about not being angry at God." Roxanne looked at him and said, "Well, I'm not angry but the God I know could handle my anger if I was." They had just found out that they were going to have to give Sunni Anne back to her birth parents and she died in her sleep the next morning. It was clear that God was saying, "You're going to know where she is."

Growing up in a Christian home, I somehow had come to believe that because I was God's child, He would protect me. Like He was an invisible shield that separated me from anything bad that could hurt me or my family.

It took Anna's diagnosis for me to take a closer look at the Bible. God had not promised to be my insurance policy, but He had promised to be with me through the trials in my life. Isaiah 43:2-3 says: "When you pass through the waters, I will be with you; and when you pass through the rivers, they will not sweep over you. When you walk through the fire, you will not be burned; the flames will not set you ablaze. For I am the LORD, your God, the Holy One of Israel, your Savior."

It's true. God has faithfully walked by my side through the rivers and the fire. Through Anna's CdLS, Joel's asthma and my own chronic fatigue.

My trials have not slipped past the defense shield. Nor are they a punishment for some sin I committed in the past. A child with special needs is a gift, not a sentence. My child is a chance to learn what true love is, because love isn't always perfect, pure or easy.

However, in the middle of the hard stuff, it's easy to think that my problems are more overwhelming than everyone else's. But when I pitch my "poor me" pity party, God has a way of reminding me to put my eyes on Him instead of my circumstances. He hasn't left my side. And it's my choice not to let a negative prognosis shake my faith.

When Adam's pancreas shut down and he was at death's door, Sherilyn was physically exhausted after days in the hospital and discouraged by the doctor's prognosis. "This is what it looks like when kids die. They don't die of cancer. They die of complications. All of a sudden, I wasn't looking at Jesus' hand holding the hand that was holding the knife. I was thinking, 'You're going to let my son die.' I was looking at the circumstances and I had it out with God. Later, when I was back on track, I was able to say, 'Lord, once again, I need to trust in You. Whether he lives or he dies, it's going to be okay. I know that you love us and you love Adam and I know the eternal perspective about this is bigger than if he lives or dies. We're going to give it to You.'"

Lisa recalled the day she was sitting on the bathroom floor bawling and yelling, "I can't do this anymore! I can't do this." Her son, Spencer, stood up and came over. He grasped her face in his hands, wiped the tears away, actually looked at her and said, "Mom, it's going to be okay." Lisa then knew that Spencer was who God had made him to be. Because there were areas where she could help him become the best he could be, she realized, "I'm just supposed to depend on God and walk and be obedient. This persevering is building character in me and this character will give hope. That's when I started looking at it in a different perspective."

A few weeks later, Lisa felt strongly that God was saying that He was healing her son. "I got so excited thinking, 'What does that mean? No more autism.' And, as I looked further into it, I realized that God's healing isn't always what we think healing is.

He was already healing me and healing my son, but that doesn't mean no autism. I don't know what it means. I just need to walk in obedience every day and take each day at a time."

When Linda went to the airport to pick up her brother after Thom had died, she "met an old foul-mouthed woman and my thought was why God would take my pure son and leave this old piece of trash. No sooner had I thought this but I realized that Thom was ready and this woman was not."

Do you think you're the only person who has ever questioned God and wrestled through the pain? Nothing you could ever say is going to shock God. He's heard it all. From those who feel God abandoned them. Whose faith died along with their dreams for a healthy, normal child. Who want to place blame.

One such parent said, "We went from being in total control to being totally out of control. We had no place to go but down – down on our knees before God. We could do nothing but hit the floor, and that's what we did. There were times when I screamed out my pain to God. We were so powerless, we were forced to go to Him. He was our only hope."[xxviii]

Honest conversations with God can move us toward hope.

Often, as in the stories above, God speaks to us though His Word as a familiar passage comes back to our memory. Here are just a few promises and reminders from a Bible full of them. As you read the following verses, let His hope and peace fill you to overflowing.

- Isaiah 41:10: "So do not fear, for I am with you; do not be dismayed, for I am your God. I will strengthen you and help you; I will uphold you with my righteous right hand."
- Joshua 1:5: "As I was with Moses, so I will be with you; I will never leave you or forsake you."
- Isaiah 42:16: "I will lead the blind by ways they have not known, along unfamiliar paths I will guide

them . . . I will not forsake them."

- Hebrews 13:5b: "Never will I leave you; never will I forsake you."

- Lamentations 3:19-23: "I remember my affliction and my wandering, the bitterness and the gall. I well remember them, and my soul is downcast within me. Yet this I call to mind and therefore I have hope: Because of the Lord's great love we are not consumed, for his compassions never fail. They are new every morning; great is your faithfulness."

- Psalm 147:11: "The Lord delights in those who fear Him, who put their hope in his unfailing love."

- Psalm 42:5: "Why are you downcast, O my soul? Why so disturbed within me? Put your hope in God, for I will yet praise him, my Savior and my God."

- Psalm 107:28-30: "Then they cried out to the Lord in their trouble, and he brought them out of their distress. He stilled the storm with a whisper; the waves of the sea were hushed. They were glad when it grew calm, and he guided them to their desired haven."

- John 16:33b: "In this world you will have trouble. But take heart! I have overcome the world."

- Psalm 57:1: "Have mercy on me, O God, have mercy on me, for in you my soul takes refuge. I will take refuge in the shadow of your wings until the disaster has passed."

- Job 11:18: "You will be secure, because there is hope; you will look about you and take your rest in safety."

- Psalm 73:26: "My flesh and my heart may fail, but God is the strength of my heart and my portion forever."

- Psalm 46:1: "God is our refuge and strength, an ever-present help in trouble."

- Psalm 130:5-6: "I wait for the Lord, my soul waits, and in his word I put my hope. My soul waits for the Lord more than watchmen wait for the morning."

- Psalm 62:5-6: "Find rest, O my soul, in God alone; my hope comes from Him. He alone is my rock and my salvation; he is my fortress, I will not be shaken."

- Psalm 69:16-17: "Answer me, O Lord, out of the goodness of your love; in your great mercy turn to me. Do not hide your face from your servant; answer me quickly, for I am in trouble."

- Hebrews 10:23: "Let us hold unswervingly to the hope we profess, for he who promised is faithful."

- Philippians 4:6-7: "Do not be anxious about anything, but in everything, by prayer and petition, with thanksgiving, present your requests to God. And the peace of God, which transcends all understanding, will guard your hearts and your minds in Christ Jesus."

People who love and trust God in the good times, learn to also trust Him in the bad times. Even though they might get tired and question why they are going through the trials, they can always have hope that God will see them through. All Job knew was that he served a righteous God who cared for him, and he would forever trust the Lord, no matter what happened in his life. Our hope is in a Savior who is worthy of our trust.

Hope causes our faith to grow into a tenacious faith that is unwilling to quit. We learn to have an unshakable trust in God and a loyal love for Him. Our growing faith is evidenced through our prayers. We go from passively praying for a child's health during a bout of pneumonia to storming the gates of heaven when told our child can never participate in physical activities. We have nothing to lose by asking, yet everything to gain.

Shannon and Ray have always prayed healing for Noah. "We feel that God is going to heal Noah, but it is going to be in His timing. So, we just pray for him and we see the healing that has already taken place. God just continues to show Himself through all of this." Lori prays for Lucas' progress and that he will have a happy life. I have prayed for Anna to develop to the fullest of her God-given potential – and she is amazing us with what she can do. My husband has prayed for Anna's vision – and her glasses prescription gets better every visit.

Every once in a while, Jan reflects on how far she has come in the journey. "Thank you God for everything that I've gone through because I would not trade where I am today. For every tear that has been shed and every blessing that I have. I'm looking forward and I'm hopeful. My faith in Christ has deepened. I know there are a lot of challenges ahead – but no matter if Kaylee lives or dies or becomes immobilized or passes away quickly or doesn't – it doesn't matter anymore because I know that I have been blessed."

Linda had been concerned about the members of their church who had stood by them and prayed for Thom's complete healing. She did not want them to be discouraged if God healed Thom by taking him home to heaven. Then another young woman in the church who had also been battling cancer took a turn for the worse and was not expected to live. Linda said, "Just before her home going, she told her parents … listen … can you hear them? There are angels all around my room. I can see them. Then she died, praising God and worshipping Him. The church was strengthened by this testimony and was able to come to terms with Thom's home going as well."

I've heard it said that laughter is the language of hope. Why? Because we moan and cry and pray for help. And, then, because we hold on to hope, we are eventually able to laugh again, even in the dark places. Our hope is God Himself. He has promised to walk beside us no matter what difficulties we face here on earth – and to bring us home to heaven to live with him for eternity. Because we know our ultimate destination, we can face the hazardous parts of the journey with courage and strength . . . and a cheerful heart ready to laugh.

If the emotional tailspin of juicing was compared to a roller coaster, then our God of hope is the seatbelt on the roller coaster. With God doing the worrying and handling the details, there's not much left to do except enjoy our kids.

In Your Kitchen

1. Pick one of the verses in the chapter that encouraged you. Write it out. Post it in a place you will see it daily. Memorize it. Think about it until it gets deeps into your soul and hope grows.

2. List times along the journey when you knew God was with you, leading you or strengthening you.

3. If you need to have it out with God, do so. Be honest. Pour out your pain and frustration. Then, let His love and peace surround you.

6 - ADDING WATER

I read about one family who had a set of quadruplets, but, due to their extremely premature births, each of the babies had to be resuscitated and developed different issues as a result.

When she was four weeks old, Samantha experienced retinopathy and laser surgery was recommended. After the surgery, the doctor informed them, "Samantha may not have vision." Years later, she was a busy preschooler with glasses. She had normal vision in her left eye but was legally blind in her right eye. She was a dainty girl who loved to sing and dance. When she grew up, she wanted to wear makeup and be a mommy of five, six or seven children.

Their son Adam experienced a brain hemorrhage three days after birth. As a result, he had brain damage, hydrocephalus (water on the brain) and cerebral palsy. At one year, he underwent surgery to receive a shunt to drain fluid from his brain. Years later, he used a wheelchair and a walker for mobility. He continued to experience epileptic seizures and some short-term memory issues. Adam was their singer and resident joke teller. He brought joy and laughter into their home. When Adam grew up, he wanted to be a firefighter – from a wheelchair. He dreamed big dreams.

Their second son, Mike, weighed only one pound, thirteen

ounces at birth. Years later, he was a tiny, yet spunky guy who loved Captain Hook. One might think that Mike was quiet and innocent. Yet, they knew that he had big plans for some mischievous fun.

And their third son, Danny, remained on a ventilator for nine weeks and was diagnosed with a congenital heart defect. He fought the odds to live and needed heart surgery. Years later, Danny had a heart murmur, but there were no restrictions on his physical activity. He was a gentle, compassionate child who loved to snuggle. Danny wanted to learn to play tennis, but his future goal was to become an astronaut.[xxix]

So far, our focus has been on the sour lemons and the sweet sugar. However, the main ingredient of lemonade, by volume, is water. What is the water? The typical, ordinary life that goes on all around us. Life may have brought us lemons but there are still clothes to wash, meals to prepare, homes to clean, homework to supervise, jobs to do, errands to run, carpools to drive, lawns to mow, children to tuck in, friends to visit, movies to see, games to play, vacations to take, families to love and dreams to dream. The sheer volume of life dilutes the lemons.

Another way to look at the water is to realize that our child and life are more normal than they are different or difficult. Sometimes, we are so focused on the momentous circumstances, behaviors and conditions that we lose sight of the person underneath.

There has been a cultural movement within the population with special needs toward "people first" language. It is a matter of semantics that reverses the tendency to look at the problem first and not the person. For example, instead of a Downs child, one would say a child with Down syndrome. Instead of an albino, we say a person with albinism. Instead of a dwarf, we say a person with dwarfism. Instead of a retarded girl, I have a daughter with mental retardation.

Some get obsessive to the point of militant activism over the language. Others still put the condition first simply to save time and words. Without debating the use of language, the underlying theme is valid. My child, and yours, is a wonderful person with needs, likes, activities, behaviors and dreams like every other child on the planet. My child's disability is a reality but it is only one part of who she is. Her condition does not define her. There is more "normal" about my child than "abnormal" and I need to pay attention.

A baby with a newly diagnosed disability is still a baby with typical baby needs. As new parents with new babies, our job is to recover from the excitement and trauma of birth. To eat and sleep. To fall in love with each other. We do what parents do with a new baby: love him, feed him, diaper him, bathe him, care for him and rest.

We spend hours holding the tiny package that fits so naturally into the crook of our arm. Rubbing our noses over their sweet-smelling fuzzy hair and watching their chests rise and fall with each breath. Counting their tiny toes and letting their fingers wrap around ours while we sing them silly songs. No matter the issues, our baby is as helpless and demanding as every other child, needing to be fed, bathed, changed and held.

Even covered in tubes, Rob could be held by his father. Roxanne said, "Tony really bonded with Rob when he put him on his shoulder. We didn't just hold him like china."

I remember holding Joel for the first time. Clint wheeled me down the hall to the nursery and I peeked into his bed and could hardly see him for all of the tubes. Still, the nurse helped straighten them out and I held Joel in my arms and watched him sleep and breathe. He was so precious and I looked past the tubes to see my baby.

As they grow, our children are still adorable and precious as they reach to attain each developmental milestone. I remember

Anna's determined look as she crawled army-commando style across the floor. I smile whenever I think of my little girl with her dark eyes framed by the longest eyelashes ever, dressed like a doll with teeny-tiny shoes, wearing a big grin as she cruised around the living room pushing an empty box.

Then there are the typical steps of children learning to talk, to dress themselves and eventually potty-training. Even if it takes longer than normal, the achievement is still celebrated and accidents still happen. After Lisa's struggles potty-training Spencer, he eventually became potty-trained also. "He has his few accidents here and there but they are normal boy accidents from playing the video games too long."

Our children are typical children with physical needs to be met and skills to master.

Our children are also typical when it comes to their favorite foods, toys and obsessions. Most children run for the ice cream truck and wrinkle their nose at a pile of broccoli. They could live on a menu of hot dogs, grilled cheese sandwiches and macaroni and cheese. They even go through the phase of cutting off bread crusts and not wanting the foods on their plate to touch. Eventually they reach the point of preferring pizza, spaghetti and hamburgers.

When it comes to the toy box, they may like balls, stuffed animals, puzzles, music and dolls. Their favorite TV shows follow the trends of their peers with the related action figures and game sets added to the toy box. They like to sing and may know the tune before they know all of the words.

Lucas, even in high school, still likes the Yu-gi-oh cards and cartoon books. He will still watch Spider Man and likes to watch a DVD of Fleetwood Mac and pretend that he is Fleetwood.

Rob is fascinated with submarines. He is an avid reader. He also loves to volunteer and helps with children's church after having taken the required training. He has a heart for missions and has been on 4 trips – two outside the country without his family along.

Noah loves anything to do with firemen, policemen, EMTs and trains. Shannon said, "That is all he talks about. That is all he is interested in. That's all he checks out at the library. Every birthday party is a fireman party and every Halloween he dresses up like a fireman."

In case Noah's obsession seems out of place, consider this. My son Luke loved construction trucks for years until I put a stop to buying more. Every book, video, clothing item, poster, toy and game he played revolved around trucks – until he switched to football with equal devotion. My son Joel loves fire trucks. He dresses up in his helmet and coat and pushes his fire trucks around the house while making siren noises. One of my nephews was obsessed with dinosaurs and knew every single type, had his room wallpapered in them, wanted a dinosaur party and built a skeleton model for his room.

What do kids like to do? Ride bikes, swim, play video games, run races, swing and slide, play tag or hide-and-seek, jump rope and color pictures. On hot summer days, they like water fights and squirt guns. They may play "pretend" inventing games with pirates, cowboys, explorers or even just playing house. Anna loves to play hide-and-seek with her collection of balls when no one else is interested in playing with her. Noah rides his bike, being a policeman and giving out tickets.

Lucas plays percussion in the school band. Lori remembered watching his first band concert in 5th grade and being amazed at how well he did, especially with his hypersensitivity to sounds. In high school, Lori would go to band class with him to keep him focused. When it came time for the concert, Lori realized she had forgotten to tell him to stand perfectly still during a very large rest in one song. Lucas instead filled the time blowing on his papers, looking for his parents and "trying to act macho and put his leg up on something. It was so precious and most people understand him."

Rob also loves music. He started piano with a little keyboard when he was 2. He then had a kindergarten teacher who invented an elaborate story to help teach him the notes and worked on his rhythm. They would march around hitting their sticks. Now, he has started playing the trombone in addition to playing the drums, the bass and regular guitar.

Sports are also a favorite activity. Lucas played T-ball when he was small. Lori remembered one game when Lucas was playing second base. The umpire decided the base needed to be moved a little bit but Lucas was upset because he thought it was supposed to be in the original location. Lori said, "The next batter hit the ball and somebody was running toward second base. The person was trying to touch the base and Lucas was running with the base trying to put it back where it belonged in his mind."

While some kids find a spot on regular teams, Special Olympics is another opportunity for children to train and compete in a variety of events. In some sports, the athletes play with partners to make it more like a game. Lucas and his brother Josh have played together for years, playing baseball, soccer, floor hockey and basketball.

Johnny was also involved in Special Olympics, starting with track and eventually participating in Frisbee, softball, golf and bowling. Gene said "Johnny always had a great deal of natural ability and a strong sense of wanting to achieve, and watching him enter in these events simply reinforced what I already knew about him."[xxx]

Noah loves to swim, swims 2 to 3 hours a week and competes in Special Olympics. Shannon said, "That's where he finds that he can be successful. My other two sons are very athletic and are always involved in sports. This way Noah found his niche and he does really well."

We are in a similar situation with our son Luke playing, and excelling at, football, basketball and baseball. Anna didn't have an athletic outlet until we signed her up for Special Olympics. The track team became a place for her to be active, train, have a uniform and compete as well as be rewarded with medals and ribbons for her efforts. She wore a perpetual smile through the whole Summer Games and we looked forward to the next sports of bowling and basketball.

Another area in which children are all the same is in their behavior. Tattling, whining, sibling rivalry, stubbornness, and disobedience are just a few behaviors seen in all children. Children with disabilities are no more pure of spirit than any other child. They are as prone to anger, selfishness, greed and spite as their non-disabled peers.

Unfortunately, the rules are often different for kids with disabilities, especially mental disabilities. Sometimes they are held to ideal standards of behavior and are never allowed to make bad choices. Why shouldn't they be free to be sloppy or rude like all other children? Instead we should use common sense and see our children in the context of humanity. What is typical behavior for children this age? If there is a problem, what part does the disability play and what part is just being a kid?

Shannon remembered one vacation when Noah was six. "I remember Ray and I just looking at each other and saying, 'We need to tell him to be quiet.' But we laughed, because we never thought we'd get to the point where we needed to tell Noah to be quiet. We had gone from his never being able to talk or be intelligible to now talking too much!"

All children also have the tendency to say things that embarrass us until we can teach them manners and what not to say. Lori said, "Sometimes you see your kid and you know it's coming. It's too late and it's going to come out. I remember one incident where there was a woman who was really heavy. Lucas looked at her and then he looked at me. I thought, Oh no! Please, don't. He said, 'Wow, she's really big.' Thank you son."

Looking back at Thom's life, Linda said he had a full life, even if it was compressed into nine years. She said, "Many funny times cheered us. Thom loved to tell jokes and make us laugh." Then, there was the day that Keith forgot to fill the tank and Linda and Thom ran out of gas on the on-ramp to the busiest freeway in Los Angeles. Linda glided the car to the curb through five lanes of traffic and then they walked to the nearest gas station. After convincing the attendant they were honest and borrowing a gas can to fill their car, they eventually got home. Linda said, "I didn't need to say a word as Thom proceeded to lecture his father about leaving the fuel nearly empty. Although we were not stranded long, the lecture no doubt left lasting memories with us all."

All children have basic emotional needs as well. They need love and security, hugs and kisses, playtime and bedtime stories, and Band-Aids on their "owies." They can smile, laugh, make friends, spread joy, play games, have fun, talk and be a friend. Children with special needs are no different. Just like the rest of us, they can feel deeply and want to form meaningful relationships. To go out and make friends. To learn and be challenged.

We can help our children develop friendships. It is common for mothers of special needs children to visit their child's class at school and answer questions. One goal of these visits it to help the other kids see how much they have in common. Do they all like ice cream? Have they ever been hurt and had to go to the hospital? Have they ever had to work hard to learn a new skill? These types of discussions help tear down walls.

Back in Wisconsin, Lori would go to Lucas' class and talk to the students about what it was like to be a person with autism. She explained that what Lucas really needed was for somebody to say hello to him. She explained why he did some of his weird things and answered every question the kids had. As a result, the other students took Lucas in and invited him to birthday parties and made him a part of their circle of friends.

As our children get older, we can help them meet new friends and participate in activities like going to the movies or having a movie night with boxes of pizza.

Appreciation can come through a meaningful work situation too. Rob loves to volunteer and is willing to do the dirty jobs of cleaning up. Roxanne said, "People really appreciate a teenager that's willing to volunteer for anything. They can't believe how hard he works or how eager he is to clean things up or help them out. That gives him a lot of credibility – so even if he might say something inappropriate or not always understand everything they are trying to discuss, the fact he has such a heart for people opens doors."

Children also dream for the future and what they long to be. Rob's dream is to be a missionary with a band and spread the Word of Christ. He also is very concerned about what he is going to do. Would he be able to go to college? What would his job be? Roxanne and Tony reassure him that with his work ethic and wide variety of interests, God has a plan for him somewhere. But Rob, as typical kids do, continues to wonder and dream about the future.

When I see my child as a typical child, I begin to treat him or her in a normal way. For example, there are basic rules in life and we need to teach them to our children. I couldn't let Anna get away with hitting or biting just because she might not understand why that was wrong. I needed to deal with the issue in a "normal" way and enforce the family rules consistently.

In some ways, our children's issues require that we handle them differently. On the other hand, much of the behavior that we find challenging proves to be normal when we witness the same in our friend's children. What gets confusing is figuring out what part is typical and what is the syndrome or condition.

Lisa said, "I think you still have to discipline your children, even if they have special needs. They need to have morals taught to them and still need to have to sit up at the table and be taught basic life and social skills. Autism is a self-focused, selfish disease. Being involved in a family unit where they don't always get their way helps my boys overcome that tendency."

One aspect of a normal childhood is being assigned household chores. By finding something that Anna can do, she is able to contribute to the family as well as learn valuable life-skills for later.

At a Special Olympics team picnic, one mother shared this advice. "My doctor told me to treat Sarah (with Down syndrome) just like my other two children. He told me to take away the bottle and work on potty training with her instead of coddling her. I am so glad that I did!"

As we treat our children as the typical children they are, we uphold the same expectations of behavior and work ethic that we apply to their siblings. By doing so, we push them to achieve and expect them to do the things they are capable of doing. Anna still tries to get me to load her backpack or help put on her shoes – but I know that she is able to do it and I don't give in. The opposite of this is a "learned helplessness" where children believe they have to have help to accomplish even the most basic tasks.

Roxanne is proud of the fact that Rob works hard to achieve his full potential. "He is maximizing and using everything that he has. There are a lot of kids that don't work to their full potential, even if they are gifted in areas, but Rob is really an overachiever in some respects."

We all have gifts and weaknesses. It is part of life that some things are easy and some are hard. We teach our children to keep working until they get it done. Perseverance is a skill that we can teach.

Problem solving is another skill we can teach our children by allowing them to experience the natural consequences of their actions. What if Anna grew up and left home and had never once been out in the cold without her mittens? My job is not to prevent and solve all of her problems, but to give her an opportunity to experience those problems and solve them for herself. Even if I could control everything in her life, to do so would fail to let her grow.

There is a struggle between our concern for their safety and our child's need to take risks. Those experiences help them develop the skills they need to eventually live without us. Our challenge is to balance protection and risk – remembering that risk is essential to learning and is a part of life for everyone. I could isolate Joel from all of his asthmatic triggers but that would deny him the experiences of life on his grandparents' acreage and helping with chores. Instead, I'm teaching him how to monitor his own condition and tell me if he needs his "breathing medicine."

The actual incidents and events involved in raising a child with a disability, if taken one at a time, are not so different from those involved in raising any child. The difference is the duration, frequency and intensity of those events multiplied by the number of issues involved.

The things that sustain us and help us to thrive are the small and seemingly ordinary parts of an ordinary day. We try to focus on how ordinary we are rather than always having to be in the category of special. Each child is different and we need to spend the time that each one needs. Even though we have special needs as a factor in our family, it cannot be the thing that runs our lives. Others may look at our child or situation with pity, but to us, our child is a sometimes wonderful, sometimes exasperating, but always-vital part of our family.

One way we continue to live a normal life is by going on family trips instead of staying at home. Shannon, Ray and their three boys take road trips to national parks like Yellowstone, Yosemite, Mt. Rushmore and the Grand Canyon as well as trips to Oregon to visit other family members. Their kids have all grown up in the car. Noah loves to camp and doesn't mind getting dirty.

Lori said, "We have made sure that we do as many normal things as we possibly can. When the kids were about 5 or 6, I realized that we couldn't wait forever to go on vacation. Now, we usually go camping to some National Park. I think it's been good for Lucas to just do those normal things." They also do road trips to visit family in other parts of the country.

Lisa's family lives on one pastoral income and can't afford to go on big vacations. But they still travel. They bought a car with a DVD player in it that helps Spencer and Jesse make transitions by capturing their attention on a video. "They love to go 'long bye-byes' and they have both asked to go to the beach this year. Hopefully, we can figure something out and take them. They are both huge Mickey Mouse fans and we are hoping in the next year or two to be able to take them to Disney World. That's our goal trip."

When a child is diagnosed with special needs, the life of the child and family will change. For some, that change is scary and we resist it. Yet, the sooner we make the necessary changes and realign our expectations, the sooner we find a new normalcy in life.

Life may be different from what you expected or planned and it can sometimes be quite difficult and painful. But life goes on and days continue to carry their richness. You can still experience the important things like the smell of a baby's neck, the sight of a colorful sunset over the mountains or the taste of ice cream with chocolate sauce. Nothing can take away the gentle breeze or a note in music. Nothing can separate you from the love of God and the world He created.

One day you will find yourself unhappy over a torn fingernail or a rained-out golf game. You will see a revival of old interests or pursuits that were pushed into the background. That is the day you realize that you have returned to the ordinary world and your child's disability is taking its place as one part of your life instead of consuming it. Life begins to take on a more balanced feel.

Life goes on and its demands water down the sour lemons and sweet sugar.

What if there are other children in your family? They add their own flavor to the mixture much like strawberries do to lemonade.

In Your Kitchen

1. List the things your child has in common with other kids and humanity in general. Include likes, dislikes, behaviors, emotional needs, activities, heroes and dreams.

2. Compare this list with the list of lemons from Chapter 1. Which is longer? Why?

7 - ADDING OTHER FRUIT

Take a quick look through the section of recipes in the back of this book. There you will find several versions of traditional lemonade that vary in sweetness or tartness. Traditional lemonade is always a pale yellow color. There's nothing wrong with basic lemonade but what if we had other fruit in the house? Strawberries, raspberries, cherries, blackberries, oranges and watermelon are just a few of the other ingredients we can add. Their addition changes the flavor and color of our lemonade.

Our child with the lemons may not be the only child in our family or the only child with lemons. The unique combinations of personalities, needs, likes and dreams create an endless variety of families. When you add the dynamic of birth order tendencies and age differences, siblings add other flavors and colors to the family batch of lemonade.

When we have a child with extraordinary needs, our focus tends to linger on them. But, the other children in the family have needs and concerns too and we need to be aware of them.

We might worry about how autism or mental retardation or asthma affects our other children. We want all of our kids to grow up as normally as possible and not have to live in a home full of stress when everything centers around a lemon situation.

Our other children also have extraordinary needs. They need extra support to live with things they can't understand and reassurance about their own physical and emotional health. They need us to listen carefully to their worries and concerns. They need clear guidelines about what they are responsible for and yet still have the freedom of childhood. They deserve to have their feelings acknowledged and help to sort out their dilemmas. They need appreciation for their sacrifices and contributions. Most of all, they need love.

The process of making lemonade in a family also affects the siblings. To add the other fruit, it may need to be juiced, cut or pureed. Our other children experience grief and loss just like the adults – losing a playmate, losing parents' attention, and losing other friends who stay away out of fear, ignorance or embarrassment. They may feel neglected because their brother or sister takes up so much time and money. They may feel burdened with higher expectations on their behavior and extra responsibilities within the family. They may become embarrassed at their sibling's behavior in public.

On the other hand, siblings are tremendous helpers and can often reach out to their brother or sister in ways the parents cannot. They can take pride in being a part of the solution and celebrate achievements. Many develop enormous patience and learn to embrace diversity. When they grow up, they may pursue careers to help others because of the empathy they have learned.

The families we have been journeying with also have siblings mixed in. Their individual experiences illustrate this wide variety of emotions, actions and benefits that encompass siblings of a child with special needs.

When Anna was just 6 months old, and long before she was diagnosed with Cornelia de Lange syndrome, I discovered that I was pregnant again. I admit that I cried for awhile because I felt so unprepared as a mother to handle another baby when I was just learning with the first. God knew what He was doing because Luke was the best thing that could have happened for Anna.

Anna needed a playmate and friend – Luke became her partner in crime as they grew up as almost twins. Luke was a development-pushing role model for Anna. She took her first steps alone just weeks before he did but the rest of her milestones came after his. For example, Luke's first word was "uh-oh" and he repeated it over and over as he purposely dropped things. Anna's first word was "ooo-oh" with the same singsong intonation. As they grew older, I heard Luke often say something like, "Anna, say pig. Can you say pig? P-p-p-ig." Then, "Good job, Anna. You said pig. Now, can you say dog?" He was like her private, round-the-clock speech therapist. Although Anna was older, Luke took on many first-born tendencies in their relationship.

Now, Anna is enjoying her role as big sister to Joel. Of course, that role includes bossing him around and tattling when he does something wrong. The rest of the time, they play together like best friends since developmentally they are closer to each other than either is to Luke.

Lori's boys Lucas and Josh had a similar experience. Lori said, "Josh was probably the best therapy we could have bought, having him for Lucas. Josh is Lucas' best friend and really his only friend." Josh will make Lucas play and go out to do things instead of staying inside. Lori said, "Josh is such a jabberbox that it makes Lucas talk too." As the youngest child, Josh is now the one looking out for his older brother if they are left alone for a brief time. "It's really Josh who is watching out and making sure that Lucas is okay and stays on track."

And yet, they are brothers and can argue like brothers. Lucas likes things in organized, orderly ways and prefers quiet. Josh, on the other hand, is not quiet, is not organized and is not orderly.

They no longer share a room! Josh understands but still gets frustrated when he can't do some things he wants to or when he has to do a chore that Lucas isn't capable of doing. Sibling rivalry still exists.

Lisa's family has a unique situation with two children with autism. Jesse's birth allowed Spencer the blessing of getting to be an older brother instead of the baby of the family. When they learned that Jesse also was on the autism spectrum, it was hard on Lisa but good for Spencer. Jesse communicates more and yet speaks Spencer's language. He pulls Spencer out and almost acts like an interpreter for his brother. Lisa and Rick saw a surge in their development together and say the brothers have an incredible relationship.

On the other hand, there are two older children in the family also affected. Lisa said, "It's been really hard for them. Yet, Joseph (then age 15) is a huge blessing to me. He has a gift of being able to handle them. He has a compassion for them and wants to include them in his life. My daughter Sophie loves to play with them and is able to connect with them in a way that is amazing too."

Sophie struggled some with the fact there are certain things that you can't do when you have special needs in your family. There are limitations and that is hard on a child. She also had trouble being the middle child, especially in a family with special needs. Lisa wanted to give her the attention she needed but Sophie was away at school during the day and their evenings were engulfed in dealing with the younger boys. So, Lisa pulled Sophie out of school and home schooled her for a year and a half. That time was a bonding time in the mother-daughter relationship and Sophie found a better understanding of where she fit in the family dynamic.

Lisa told her older kids, "You have been given a gift and a perspective that most people don't have. You have special needs in your family and you have been given understanding."

In Sherilyn's family, the sibling dynamic was different. David was older than his stepbrothers and at first struggled with losing the attention that had been his. Later, he struggled with the comparisons. Daniel, who was 9 ½ years younger than David, actually walked down the stairs without holding on sooner than David did. Adam, even younger, could pitch a real-sized basketball into a small, lowered hoop at 18 months of age. Sherilyn said, "It's one thing if people out there are doing things, but it's another if it's your little brothers who are doing things that even you can't do." With cerebral palsy, David couldn't physically do things as well but mentally he understood that there was a ten-year age difference and he struggled with that realization.

The sibling comparisons are also present with Rob and his younger brother Casey. Although separated by 19 months in age, Casey used to help Rob with his 5th grade math homework. One day, Rob turned to Casey and said, "You don't even need to go to 5th grade next year because you already know all this stuff." Later, when the teachers recommended that Casey skip 5th grade, Roxanne and Tony were able to tell Rob that he had the idea first and asked what he thought about it. The brothers have been in the same grade since 6th grade but are placed in different classes.

The difficulty in comparisons comes from Casey's perspective. The way Casey explains it is, "Rob does a 7 or 8 (on a scale of ten) and everyone is cheering and it's great. I dip down to a 9 and I'm in trouble." Roxanne agrees that it is probably true because Rob could be doing a 3 or 4 but has worked really hard to get to a 7 or 8. On the other hand, Casey may or may not have worked at all to get to a 9 on the scale.

Casey first realized something was different about Rob when he was young. He would ask, "Mom, why is it so easy for me to pump the swing and that's still something that is hard for Rob to do? And he's bigger than I am." As they grew up, Casey was Rob's defender, even though he was years younger than those teasing his brother. Now, while trying to negotiate his own way through adolescence with peers who are older than he is, Casey still tries in his own way to advocate for Rob. "But," Roxanne said, "he can't always figure out how to deal with the curveballs Rob throws him."

Noah's autistic temper tantrums have improved as he has

gotten older but they still can make things really difficult for the rest of the family and his brothers Nick (4 years older) and Casey (16 months younger). Shannon said, "They don't look at Noah as being different until a situation arises. They get upset with Noah and we have to remind them about what Noah is dealing with and that he doesn't process information the way they do."

While Nick and Casey don't feel bitterness about their parents spending so much time with Noah or that Noah needs this or that, they do get frustrated when they miss out on activities. For example, the family went to Denver for a weekend trip. When away from home and his routine, everything has to be Noah's way in an attempt to avoid blowups. Unfortunately, blowups happened and the brothers were frustrated that Noah was ruining their weekend. Sometimes the family just lets Noah have his way in order to get him to calm down. While Nick understands that it is necessary to remedy the situation, Casey just feels, "Why does he always get his way?"

The brothers also get embarrassed when Noah acts out. One time, they all went to Wendy's for supper. A bunch of high school kids came in and Nick, who was 15, was very aware of everyone who was around. Noah started having a fit because he wanted a Frosty and was pulling his hair and putting his shirt over his face. Nick was sinking down in his chair with embarrassment and said, "I'm going to go to the car." It can be embarrassing to see a ten-year-old child behaving that way.

For the most part, Nick is not embarrassed by Noah and he includes him. Casey and Noah also play really well together. And, sometimes, Casey will go out of his way to do something really nice for Noah. One morning, Casey set up all of the fire trucks in Noah's room and, on the chalkboard, drew a house on fire as if the fire trucks were putting the fire out. Noah was thrilled because of his love of firemen and Casey did it because he knew that Noah would love it.

Since having a brother or sister with special needs has a

lasting impact on the other children in the family, what can we do to help our other children?

First, we can let them know it is okay to grieve the losses of their friends, expectations, time and attention. And, if they have lost a sibling or loved one, children need to know that it is okay to feel sad. God can use the adults in their lives to help bring healing and, in the process, help heal the adults' hurting hearts as well.

Here are some ways to help children deal with their loss.

- Be honest with your children.

- Use age-appropriate language to help them understand what is happening.

- Listen to their fears, hurts, anger and concerns.

- Learn to use words that encourage them to talk about their feelings. "How does that make you feel?" "Do you want to talk about it?" "Is there anything I can do to help you feel better?" "I know you are hurting, but I'm always here for you." "It's okay to cry."

- Help children say good-bye to a person they have lost by writing a letter, writing a poem or drawing a picture.

- Celebrate the memory of the person they have lost by planting a tree, making a special garden, donating to a charity, making a scrapbook of memories, releasing balloons or flying a kite with the person's name attached to the string.

- Keep the person's picture in a place of honor.

- Talk about the person on special days, such as that person's birthday.

- Laugh and remember the good times together.

During Thom's last week of life, Keith and Linda felt they needed to devote all of their time to Thom but realized that his siblings needed special time and attention too. They decided to have the siblings stay with their grandparents. "This proved to be a wise decision," said Linda. "We were able to spend unlimited and uninterrupted time with Thom. Thom's siblings had a wonderful time with their grandparents so everything worked out well."

After Thom passed away, Shelley and Troy needed Linda's attention and life went on. Linda and Keith took Thom's savings account and purchased a special pal for each of the kids as something special from Thom. Linda said, "They kept their pals for many years."

Siblings can also learn to identify and process their feelings of frustration or embarrassment through a sibling support group. These groups are designed for children to be able to discuss their feelings with other children facing similar situations. In finding common ground, they are able to get ideas and move forward.

When Casey joined a sibling support group, Roxanne wasn't sure what he should tell people about Rob. Rob's mosaic Down syndrome was a difficult thing to understand and communicate, especially when you are seven years old. People reassured Roxanne that Casey would know what to say. So, when he went the second time Casey said, with Rob sitting beside him in the car, "Last time they asked us to go around and say what was wrong with our brother or sister. I couldn't think of anything except that you had already had 4 or 5 sets of PE tubes and that you were in speech therapy. But I didn't tell them about my set of PE tubes or my speech therapy."

What bugged Casey for years was that he had the same tubes in his ears and speech therapy, but there was something different. It was harder for Rob to do things than it was for Casey but he didn't fully understand why that was. Roxanne thought that Casey held onto guilt about that even into his teen years.

Children, like Casey, may know that there is a difference between themselves and their brother or sister, but not be able to describe it or understand it. We need to teach the siblings about the condition at a level they can understand – and revisit the conversation as they get older and begin to process information differently.

Whenever we attended a Cornelia de Lange syndrome conference or family gathering, Luke was exposed to others with CdLS. Through the years, it has been interesting to see how his views have changed. He began to ask a lot of questions about Anna and what made her different, even from the others with CdLS that he met. Those conversations deepened his understanding of his sister and made him more patient. At least, until we got back into the reality of our regular lives and she became his annoying sister again.

Lori has also had the opportunity to educate and talk with her son Josh about his older brother Lucas. They once watched an Oprah special on autism and cried together. Josh opened up and was able to tell his mom that it was really hard sometimes because Lucas' behavior would embarrass him. Josh, when he was 9, also attended a sibling group through the Autism Society. It was a fun chance for him to do things with other kids but the purpose was to help siblings of children with disabilities try to understand what was going on in their lives.

Another way to reach out to your non-disabled children is to make special time for them whenever possible. It doesn't have to cost a lot of money or take a lot of time, but children need special, undivided attention from their parents. It also makes a great opportunity for a parent to find out how things are really going in their lives and help process their feelings. Although we don't have regularly scheduled times, I do try to spend one-on-one time with all three of my kids, Anna included, connecting with them. I can certainly tell by Luke's behavior when we are overdue for some Mommy time.

Shannon and Ray "date" their sons Nick and Casey with individually scheduled times. For example, Ray will take Nick to breakfast every Thursday morning. Shannon said, "We've always been very careful to do that so that they don't feel left out. That's helped a ton! Some kids can get very resentful. It could happen easily because Noah needs so much attention." Growing up, Nick and Casey spent hours in the car on the hour drive to Noah's speech therapy. They did it because it had to be done and they didn't complain.

So far, we have added lemon juice, sugar, water and other fruit. Now it's time to start stirring!

In Your Kitchen

1. Run a mental check to see whether your expectations for each of your children are reasonable and in balance. Is each child getting most of what he or she needs most of the time?

2. Plan a one-on-one time with each child. Use that time to reconnect, have fun and talk about how things are going. Ask if they have any ideas to make things go more smoothly at home.

3. Hug each of your children and let them know how important they are in your family.

8 - STIRRING LEMONADE

"We read everything we could find on cancer and talked to everyone to get a general view of what was ahead," said Linda. "Thom's stomach swelled to twice the size and we had to purchase men's pants and shorten them for him to wear. He spent many nights in the hospital getting him stabilized and I always stayed too. The doctors were sympathetic but had no answers for us."

"About that time, a couple of parents gave us a book on one person's journey with cancer. It talked about the fact that chemo and other procedures were poisons meant to stop all new cell growth. It explained that this was not the only treatment available but that the medical establishment only wanted to use expensive poisons instead of other viable procedures," said Linda. "Now, we were in a quandary. Which way was the best one to treat him and what should we do?"

Simply having lemon juice, sugar and water isn't enough. They have to be mixed together and the most common tool used is a spoon. Similarly, we mix the sour experiences, water of life and sugar of hope by putting our faith into action. We first find out everything we can about the problem and find out what things we can do for our child. Then we roll up our sleeves and start stirring. We do what we can and leave the results in God's hands.

James wrote about this unique balance between faith and action. He said, "Faith by itself, if it is not accompanied by action, is dead."[xxxi] He went on to say, "I will show you my faith by what I do."[xxxii]

I sometimes hear on the news about a family who, believing that God was going to heal their child, refused simple medications or interventions. I firmly believe that God, who created our minds in His image to be both capable and creative, has allowed mankind to discover the healing benefits of antibiotics and the technological advances of imaging machines and surgeries. I believe that denying the use of these methods is to deny the hand of the Creator working through His creation. I believe in at least exploring all of the options.

Accepting the reality of our situation does not mean that we sit idly by and do nothing. We cope by getting busy and working to make the best of our situation. There aren't easy answers or quick solutions. Instead, we have to wade through volumes of advice, information and research to decide what we want and what we are willing to do to achieve it. Then, it is up to us to pick up the spoon and start stirring.

Rather than being offered information and guidance about their child, many parents have to seek it out themselves. They play medical detective at a time when their emotional lives are in upheaval. Yet, the search for information is an alternative to feeling helpless and hopeless. It is our effort to stay busy and to uncover any treatment or intervention that might help at the same time. It satisfies our need to take some kind of action. If we are filled with hope, it affects our determination to seek out anything that might help.

A lot of answers are out there to be found if we know where to look. We learn our first information from the doctors or specialists working with our child. That tidbit of information at the time of diagnosis satisfies initially until more questions arise on the way home. Soon, we are searching the library and the Internet for every book, article or piece of information we can find. We read Web postings from parents like us.

The first information we find might not be very helpful or hopeful. The first book Lori read on autism, at the recommendation of their doctor, said to get the child into a good education plan and hope for the best. She said, "The first book I read was really depressing." I have talked to other parents of children with Cornelia de Lange syndrome who were initially told their children would never walk, never talk and would be dead within a year. That information was completely hopeless – and wrong!

Soon, we find organizations and websites dedicated to what we are researching. Lori found a lot of information through the Autism Society. She eventually went to work for them as a program coordinator, reading and reviewing books from their lending library. By meeting other parents and friends, Lori also had access through the years to over 100 conferences and trainings on special education, advocacy and autism.

I found volumes of information (and hope) through the Cornelia de Lange Syndrome Foundation. I requested every research article and publication they had. I quickly had a 4-inch thick binder full of information. My dad and I both searched other sources for information and research studies. We found that professionals closely tied to the CdLS Foundation wrote most of those other articles we found. We were getting accurate information from the source. We attended their conferences, met other families in Colorado through gatherings and I joined the Foundation as an Awareness Coordinator.

The more common the condition, the more information falls into your lap. Lisa said that people hand her articles on autism all of the time. "Everywhere you look in the news or on television, there is a link to autism. In sports, there was a story about a boy who played basketball. Even on those shows where they go into houses to fix them up, one family had a child with autism. Research studies are published and new shows are talking about the rise in autism. Everywhere you look, you find autism."

In fact, parents often want more information than doctors can offer. These parents are the driving behind many research grants, funding drives and the formation of support organizations.

We learn enough to become mini-medical specialists on our child's particular condition. We may even find ourselves in situations where we know more about the disability than the experts there to advise us. At Anna's initial genetic appointment where we received her diagnosis, we were told to return in a year for a follow-up appointment. A year later, I quickly discovered that I knew more about CdLS than the geneticist there to answer my questions. She quickly figured it out as well, excused herself for a minute and returned with three pediatric interns. They sat down and picked my brain for what I knew. I was teaching doctors the information I had gathered on a subject near to my heart.

We also need to do our research in making medical decisions. First, we research the doctor, getting recommendations from friends, family members and trusted physicians. We can even check into their standing with the medical board. Second, before our appointments, it is helpful to make a written list of all our questions and concerns. At the appointment, we ask our questions and get the answers clarified. Don't be afraid to ask for a referral to a specialist if necessary. Third, we weigh the pros and cons of any surgery or procedure before deciding if it is really necessary. Last, we can show appreciation for our doctor by keeping our appointments, being on time, following the prescribed plan and even dropping a note of thanks.

Taking the time to research medical decisions could be the difference between life and death. Don't necessarily accept one laboratory result or one doctor's diagnosis as fact. You may want to get a second opinion regarding advised surgery or extensive medical treatment.

Sometimes in the process of research, we find unexpected answers. After Lisa found out that Spencer was on the autism spectrum, she immediately went into her self-described firstborn child conquer attitude. "I jumped right in and learned all I could and continued trying to understand autism so I could help fix it. The more that I learned, I began to understand that there is a genetic disposition and maybe some environmental disability as well. It was as though there was a genetic disposition or thinking pattern of autism that was amplified by Spencer's birth issues, his mold allergy and reaction to immunizations. His immune system just couldn't handle certain things."

Lisa also learned about the thinking patterns of autism to help her communicate with her sons. "For example, instead of saying 'We're going to Blockbuster Video,' we call it Blue TV because it has a blue color and its about something on the TV. We speak in colors and shapes and numbers and different sizes. Learning their language has been the biggest help for me."

The more Lisa researched and learned about the thinking patterns of autism and its genetic aspect, she realized that this type of thinking pattern was also in her father, who struggled in society his whole life. He had a brilliant mind but was never really understood. "So in the process of understanding Spencer, I understood my father. And we had about two years of an understanding father-daughter relationship before he passed away. Understanding Spencer helped me to understand my father and I was able to pass that knowledge along to his parents. They were a hardworking, farming family who hadn't understood their own son until I explained the thinking pattern. They realized that he couldn't help some of his issues. Before my dad had his bypass surgery, my grandfather went in and told him, probably for the first time ever, that he loved him just the way he was."

In addition to learning about the disease or disability, we also need to research the programs and services available. We need to learn to deal with the bureaucracy of schools, support services and welfare agencies. At a minimum, every child in the United

States is entitled by law to a free and appropriate public education. Additional services available are legal advice and advocacy, medical services, in-home assistance, specialized equipment, respite care, social and recreational activities, access to parent networks and family counseling. There are also resources available in communities through families, churches and neighborhoods.

We all search differently. Some go right to the library or computer and conduct a systematic search. Others start by asking around to find other families and pick their brains. Often, we do some of both.

Our initial search for information tapers off as we get busy implementing what we have learned. However, new stages and issues along the way send us back to the computer. There is always new research being done and new treatments being found. Staying on top of the current information is as important as finding that information in the beginning.

We research until we can answer these two questions. "What are we dealing with?" and "What is the best therapy or treatment approach?" Once we gain some distance between the problem and ourselves, we are more likely to gain perspective and see solutions. Then, we can decide on a path to take and jump back into the action.

One of the first actions we take is to educate those around us who come in contact with our child. If our child behaves inappropriately in public, uses a wheelchair or has lost their hair due to chemotherapy, we will attract attention – and not always the good kind.

Some parents take a proactive approach. When (not if) their child has an issue in public, they deal with the child's behavior and then use it as an educational experience for those standing around watching. Sometimes without saying a word, they reach into their pocket and pull out a card, resembling a business card, that contains basic information about autism or other specific conditions. They've found that a little education helps to relieve many stressful moments.

Because our children live out among people in society, they will regularly encounter people, from a new teacher to the checkout clerk at the store, who will fail to appreciate that the way they are behaving is the best that they can do. We pave the way by educating those who come in contact with our child.

Another avenue of education comes by preparing our children to deal with the world. We role-play social situations and practice appropriate responses. We teach our children how to deal with the inevitable bully. We may never be able to change other people's kids, but we can help our child learn important lessons about compassion, forgiveness, comfort in God and basic survival skills.

We can also teach our children, as they get older, to speak for themselves. Roxanne once was telling friends that they never wanted Rob to use his diagnosis of mosaic Down syndrome as a crutch. One friend said, "But he's a hard worker and he uses everything he has to do whatever job needs to be done. Instead of people expecting a 10 and he delivers an 8 and they get frustrated with him, don't you think it would be easier if you lower their expectations a little bit? It would help others understand Rob and give him the tools to explain it to others."

So, Roxanne and Tony starting having Rob do more advertisement of his condition. He would sit down with his class and say, "Here are the facts and this is what I need from you. I need it black and white. I can't deal with subtle innuendos. I don't pick up on them and don't want you to get mad at me because I missed it. You have to be really direct with me." It's a skill that will serve Rob for years as well as paving the way for understanding from his peers.

When a child has a medical condition, we also have to educate the school system and those who work with our child. Most schools have a health office and you can file a medical plan with the school nurse. When Anna was dealing with frequent episodes of acid reflux, I wrote out a plan describing in detail her symptoms and what medications should be given. One year, she had to go to the office before lunch every day for a prescription medication that I sent to school.

Adam was diagnosed with leukemia and started chemotherapy over the summer before his sophomore year of high school. Sherilyn notified the school and asked that all of the teachers be told to allow Adam to keep his cell phone with him at all times. He also had to be allowed to just get up and walk out of a classroom without talking to a teacher first because he might need to throw up. She asked that all of the teachers be notified and left it up to the counselor to follow through. In retrospect, she should have been more proactive.

On the first day of school, Adam's health teacher was telling the class about the topics they were going to be studying including diseases like cancer. He said, "If you think for a minute, I'm sure you can think of somebody you know that has cancer." One of Adam's friends piped up, "Adam has cancer." Adam said, "Yeah, I got cancer this summer."

The teacher had taught Adam the year before and knew that he loved to make people laugh. So, he said, "Knock it off. This is not something to joke around about."

He was about to send them out of the room until Adam lifted up his shirt for everyone to see. "Does this look like I'm joking around? That is a port and it goes into my heart. This is where my Mom and I are injecting chemo. This is not a joke." The teacher really liked Adam and was emotionally shaken. He had to leave the room and didn't come back for 20 minutes. The teacher shouldn't have had to find out like that nor should Adam have been put on the spot in front of the class. A little information would have helped.

One practical form of stirring involves medications, medical procedures, tests and surgeries. Kaylee is on medication to control the complex partial seizures that result from the tubers in her brain. Lucas is on anxiety medication to take the edge off and allow him to be more flexible with changes in his routine. My son Joel is on an asthma controller nebulized steroid daily in addition to his rescue bronchodilator and allergy medications. Anna was on medications to prevent her acid reflux and to heal the open sores in her stomach.

Lori's other son Josh has ADD and takes a medication to help with his concentration at school. The family can tell when he is having growth spurts and it isn't working as well. The down side of his medication is that he isn't hungry and doesn't eat or grow as he should. Lori said, "I tend to take him off in the summer and we go with whatever behavior happens. He has a little growth spurt in the summer and then we are back on it in the fall. I don't know if that's the best answer but that's what we've had to do."

Adam's treatment for leukemia involved chemotherapy drugs in both liquid and pill forms. The doctors gave them a "roadmap" schedule of which drugs were to be taken, how often he was to take them, when he was to be seen, and when blood was to be drawn. Adam took some of the drugs in pill form morning, noon and night every day. Another drug was injected but, due to vicious side effects, was followed by 8 or 10 liters of water to flush out his system. Other pills were taken to help control the nausea.

Adam had a port in his heart for the injection of some of the drugs. Sherilyn said, "He had a tube attached to it that had all these valves on it so he didn't bleed all over the floor. I would open the valve on the end, insert the needle and inject the chemo with all of the valves open so it would go into his heart. Then I would turn everything off later. Adam and I were playing nurse at home and didn't know what we were doing!"

The hospital gave Keith and Linda the medical routine they recommended for Thom and said they would start it the following week. In the meantime, they decided to go to Mexico and check out the famous Contrares Clinic in Playas. "We had heard many great things about them," said Linda. "We took him down and put him in the hospital there. A couple of hours later, we were called. Dr. Contrares asked about the routine that Children's Hospital recommended. He agreed with their plan but wanted to add Laetrile. Laetrile is natural cyanide found in apricot pits and sold at health food stores in the United States. This was considered a healthy alternative to chemo."

It was decided that Thom would take the chemo medicine in combination with a special diet that included no animal protein. Linda said, "The diet was rather radical so we decided that the entire family would eat the same way. God sent us Seventh Day Adventist neighbors, who introduced us to the many varieties of vegetarian foods." They even learned how to make Thom's favorite "Egg McMuffin" using whole-wheat muffins, wham (a ham substitute), artificial eggs and very aged cheese.

In addition to medications, there are many tests we have done to monitor our child's health. Anna had an upper endoscopy to take pictures of her esophagus and stomach and check for damage from the acid reflux. Kaylee has had numerous MRI, CAT scans and other tests to monitor the tubers in her brain and check for their development on her other organs. One such test revealed the growth of a tumor in a dangerous region of her brain. Jan negotiated for a repeat test in six months instead of a year.

Then there are the surgical interventions. Kaylee has laser surgery for the angiofibromas on her face. They will never go away but the laser surgeries keep them under control so they do not open up and bleed. Kaylee needs to have this done a couple times each year but Jan has to hold her down onto the table. It's harder to do that as Kaylee gets older and bigger.

David had two eye surgeries and needs a third. Noah had two major surgeries because of his cleft palette. He also had 4 sets of PE tubes implanted. Rob had his first set of PE tubes by 9 months of age and ended up with a new set of tubes every year for several years.

Another way we stir is through therapy. Speech therapy, occupational therapy (OT) and physical therapy (PT) may be received in the home, at a clinic or through the school system. Often, the therapists give parents additional exercises or ideas to incorporate at home during the week.

In the world of autism, the applied behavior analysis (ABA) program is now considered by many to be a mainstream treatment program. Once Noah was diagnosed with autism in California, the label got him the ABA program and tutoring in their home. Prior to that program, Shannon and Ray had paid for outside services because the school provided the bare minimum. With ABA, tutors through the school system came to their home and worked on things over and over with Noah, using repetition and reinforcement.

In Wisconsin, Lori found out about ABA from other parents in a support group. She realized that it would work for him because he learned differently, in small strict steps. She started researching the program and discovered it was really expensive. Instead, she found other families, located a man who had been trained and had different college kids and other volunteers receive training. "We put together a program for our home and started having these people come about 20 hours a week in addition to school."

When Lucas was about four, the state of Wisconsin approved ABA as a therapy for autistic children. He qualified for the Medicaid waiver because of his disability so they began to receive financial help for their ABA program. For the next seven years, "We had between 25 and 40 hours a week of one-on-one therapy in our home in addition to Lucas' going to school. So, you can imagine, that not only did it have a big impact on him, it had a big impact on everything in our life. There were always people coming and going." Since they moved to Colorado, Lori has learned that the program is not as generous as it once was because funding had been cut. "We were fortunate to be where we were at the right time and place."

One drawback to the ABA was that everything had to be specifically taught. Lori remembered Lucas bringing home a math story problem. "It said if you had so many rings and so many necklaces, how much jewelry did you have? Well, that didn't make sense to Lucas. I had never taught him that all those things were jewelry. He was a boy and he didn't need to know about jewelry. But, he couldn't do the math problem because he didn't understand. There are little things that you forgot to teach."

The key to ABA and other traditional therapies is to intervene early in the life of the child because you can still change things dramatically. This the foundational premise of the early intervention and educational programs now mandated by law. We have come a long way in the last thirty-five years since the Education for All Handicapped Children Act was passed in 1975.

Before then, children were taught – if at all – in drab, hospital-like settings without access to the latest educational materials or techniques. For most of these children, the programs turned into baby-sitting facilities without any academic progress. Some teachers and parents were ahead of their time and made groundbreaking strides to prove that children with disabilities could be taught successfully. Classroom programs expanded to include speech and occupational therapy.

When Anna was diagnosed with CdLS, we were encouraged to get speech therapy and physical therapy. I started calling around and pricing what therapy would cost. One lady I talked to asked if we had tried "Child Find" yet. Even though I was a licensed elementary teacher, I didn't know about this program.

Because of the dramatic results of early intervention, later education laws encouraged the development of programs for children with disabilities from birth to three years of age. Often the programs include education, speech therapy, OT, PT, adapted physical education and a low teacher-student ratio. We had Anna tested by our local school district and, because she was below the 7th percentile developmentally, she qualified to be in a toddler program with integrated therapies. She went to school two mornings a week and received additional therapy in our home.

It is hard to balance the importance of early intervention with family life. Roxanne, a professional speech pathologist who was a strong advocate for early intervention programs, found it very difficult to let go of Rob at an early age. She had quit work to stay home with the baby, after waiting for a child for so long, and now was being encouraged to send him to a six-hour-a-day intense therapy program. "But, I'm home to be with him, not to take him to therapy." She decided against the six-hour daily program but still cried just going to one hour of therapy each week. "I wasn't supposed to be driving to and from therapy with my two-month-old." Her professional approach to early intervention is more balanced now.

At age three, preschool programs officially begin followed by the traditional kindergarten through high school programs. Each child's needs differ, so Individualized Education Plans (IEPs) design an appropriate program for each child. Some children are fully included in the regular classroom with support services like tutoring available. Others spend most of their time in a segregated classroom with academic instruction at their level. Some programs emphasize academic skills while others focus on life skills. Still other children handle a few regular education classes with the support of a paraprofessional aide.

While it looks good on paper, sometimes the reality is that children just don't fit well into a program. For example, Lucas didn't fit into the learning disabilities, cognitive needs or emotional needs programs in their area but he couldn't handle the regular classes alone. Shannon had similar frustrations about Noah's educational situation because he didn't fit in their local special education program (that was not designed for autistic children) or the regular classroom. She considered home schooling once Noah reached middle school but made the decision to start halfway through his 5th grade year.

On the other hand, just a few miles away in the city of Fort Collins, Lisa's boys are in a class designed specifically for autistic children. Spencer and Jesse attend regular classes but are pulled out for different subjects that they wouldn't understand. Lisa said, "The school's resources to meet the needs of this group of young boys have been amazing."

As parents, we first need to study our children and understand their needs. Then we need to fight for the program they need in school and not be afraid to change it if it isn't working. There is not a program that works for every child. Decide what your goals are for your child's education and do what you need to do in order to meet them.

For example, Anna's kindergarten program was a disaster. She did not have the support she needed and often sat by herself scribbling on paper while the rest of the class listened to a story with the teacher. She didn't learn anything the whole year. The recommendation of the staff at her IEP meeting in the spring was to send her to a school with only other mentally retarded children where she could get instruction at her level. I knew Anna's tendency to imitate everything around her and did NOT want her to pick up new behaviors from non-typical peers.

We were already moving to another town and school district so I saved my fight for the next staff. In our new town, Anna qualified for a program that was the best of both worlds and was ideal for her. She was placed in a regular classroom with typical peers for social studies, science, art, music, gym, library, computers, lunch, recess, and silent reading times. She was pulled out for speech therapy, occupational therapy and adaptive physical education. She also went to another structured classroom for instruction in reading, writing and math at her level. She thrived and excelled. (The same type of program did not work for Noah because his needs are different than Anna's.)

On a positive note, her educational team diagnosed Anna's hyperlexia and then implemented a curriculum designed specifically to help her create pictures in her brain when she reads. With this additional, targeted method, she was reading "stories" made entirely of pictures before transferring her new comprehension skills back to written stories.

One last thought before we move on. Inclusion was the

buzzword for years meaning that children should spend all of their time in the regular classroom. It certainly works for some but others do not have the skills to be included. Some children with significant issues can be disruptive and pull the teacher's time and efforts from the other students in the class. Additionally, not all teachers have the training or support needed to help every child succeed in their classroom. Personally, I don't think it works for everyone and that is okay. You have to find what is best for your child.

Sometimes our stirring takes us outside the traditional avenues of medications, therapies and education. We are willing to try somewhat-unusual things hoping to help our child. If it works, great. If not, then we move on. As one parent put it, "In the early days I chose to pursue the neurological cure for autism. I also pursued the behavioral cure, the nutritional cure, the situation-management cure, the environmental cure, and the when-things-get-tough-let's-go-for-a-ride-to-see-the-power-lines cure."xxxiii

Some parents try music therapy or hippotherapy (horseback riding). Others try massage or acupuncture. With autism, Lisa learned about a dog therapy. She knew that Spencer had a connection with animals and learned from them. Although Lisa had tried to teach him before, he learned to swim after watching the "March of the Penguins" movie. The school district brought a dog into the classroom to help teach Spencer how to do things. He learned how to brush his teeth and comb his hair as a result. By taking care of an animal, it helped him realize that he needed to take care of himself.

Sometimes we try adding or removing certain foods.

Shannon and Ray tried removing a lot of dyes, wheat and gluten from Noah's diet but didn't notice a difference. They tried to add the omega-3s found in fish oil because they are supposed to help with the brain but Noah wouldn't eat it no matter how they disguised it. Who knows if it would have made a difference or not?

Lori gave Lucas enzymes for a while and tried removing dairy or gluten from his diet. "It didn't seem to make a huge difference for him or maybe I just wasn't good enough at it. I do know of families who have done that and their kids have made remarkable changes. We weren't one of them." In the process, she did learn that Lucas can't have soy because it makes him hyperactive.

Research studies on Down syndrome have found there are definite nutritional and chemical imbalances as the extra chromosome expresses itself. Roxanne started Rob on targeted nutritional supplements called Nutrivene when he was 2. He is much healthier now and rarely misses a day of school unless he is having or recovering from a surgery.

The same company has made a couple of other formulas for other syndromes including Cornelia de Lange syndrome. We tried it with Anna and noticed a dramatic increase in her health and stamina. She also began combining her vocabulary into unique sentences instead of using stock phrases like "I want a _____" or "I see a _____." After awhile, we couldn't get the powder down her anymore and the cost was prohibitive. We stopped and didn't notice any declines in her development or health. Did the nutritional supplement really make the difference or was I simply more aware of her development? I don't know.

Another time, we tried a special diet with Anna to see if there were any foods or additives affecting her behavior and development. It was a confusing and expensive experiment. I'm so thankful that my mother stepped in to do the calculating of ratios and meals. I only had to check the menu and heat up Anna's portion.

On one hand, I wanted to find an answer to help Anna. On the other hand, I hoped this wasn't it because I didn't know how our family could live like that or afford the special foods. We saw no changes as her system detoxified or as we added foods back into her diet. It works for some – just not for us.

When Rob was 9 years old and had just gotten another set of

PE tubes because of his chronic ear infections, a homeopathic doctor recommended they take Rob off of cow's milk. Roxanne put him on soymilk instead. From age 9 to 16, Rob had a total of three ear infections and three sinus infections. He could still eat ice cream, cheese and yogurt in moderate amounts and was far healthier overall. Roxanne wishes there was more research available on homeopathic remedies and their interactions with traditional medicines.

Lisa experiments to find out what foods or allergies affect her boys. She tries different things at home without telling the school the specifics. The teacher keeps a daily log of their behavior during the day so Lisa can see what is really helping them or not. She has learned and tries to eliminate mold-born foods as well as give them regular vitamin supplements. Every child is different and there isn't a magic answer when it comes to nutrition.

Here are a few other things parents have tried.

Roxanne had Rob do a computer-based program called Fast Forward one summer. He worked 1 ½ or 2 hours a day on auditory processing and reading skills. He was a strong reader but his comprehension wasn't at the level of his decoding.

With Josh's ADD, staying on task and being organized are big issues for him. Getting ready for school every morning can be a real challenge. Lori has notes posted on the door with the schedule to help him remember things. She also checks his school agenda and the homework hotline. Right now Lori is keeping him organized but is trying different strategies to help him learn to organize himself as he gets older.

Lisa got Spencer involved in an Asberger's research project at Colorado State University. He didn't really fit the mold because he didn't want to communicate but she hopes to put Jesse into a social program there. The professors from CSU visit her sons' classroom regularly and bring their students, so her children are teaching teachers how to teach kids with autism.

For Sherilyn, part of meeting David's social and emotional needs involved letting him go live with his father out of state. With the bullies and rejection at school combined with two babies in the home, David needed a change of pace. After spending a year in Kansas, David wanted to stay. So, instead of letting go of her son at age 18, she had to let go when he was almost 13. David didn't move back to live with Sherilyn until he was 27 years old.

Shannon and Ray looked for a therapy to help Noah learn to speak after he was diagnosed with dyspraxia dysarthria. They did a lot of research because there were many different approaches being used. They found the PROMPT Institute in New Mexico that used a tactile approach to speech. They planned a family trip and went out there for a week. The doctor there was the first to tell them that Noah would speak but he had to have the right therapy.

Shannon said, "She got him saying his vowel sounds within the first week that we were there. So, it was bittersweet because going home, there was no therapist in our area trained in this." They began to battle with speech therapists at home and even prayed about moving to New Mexico. "Within three weeks, she called and there was a doctor about an hour away who was trained in it. So, we started driving an hour one way twice a week to get speech therapy." Noah went from not speaking at all to speaking intelligibly. "Now he doesn't shut up!" said Shannon.

We found ourselves pursuing an unusual approach as well. A woman in our church gave us a copy of a book by Glenn Doman called *What to Do About Your Brain-Injured Child*. At first I was turned off by the title but, since she was convinced it would help Anna, I read it. His methods were developed treating stroke patients and had remarkable results in cases where traditional methods had failed. He had also found that children with Down syndrome and other genetic conditions had both a genetic component and a treatable brain-injury.

I traveled to Philadelphia to the Institutes for the Achievement of Human Potential to sit in 50 hours of lectures on diagnosing and treating specific brain injuries. I learned how to evaluate where Anna was on their chart and learned specific exercises to do to treat each area of her brain that was blocked. Taking what I learned, I developed a treatment program for Anna and determined to give it a fair shot.

The first thing that I noticed when I evaluated Anna was that her left eye turned slightly inward and did not completely contract when exposed to bright light. The prescribed treatment was sitting in a dark closet with a flashlight stimulating her left eye to react over and over during the day. We also did a lot of creeping, on hands and knees, up and down the hall. Within a few weeks, her left eye was contracting normally and no longer drifted inward.

The most controversial thing we did was something called patterning. The idea behind patterning is that the repetitive pattern of motion of arms and legs while crawling and creeping forms pathways in the brain. However, children without this regular motion on their own can have that pathway imprinted in their brain by having their arms and legs moved in the correct pattern by others. For 5 minutes at a time, 5 times a night, we moved Anna's arms and legs while she lay on a table. We did this for two weeks and then quit.

Before we started patterning, Anna was walking with her arms raised above her shoulders for balance. She had three words but spoke so quietly that you had to be within several feet of her mouth to hear her. After a few days of patterning, Anna doubled her vocabulary and you could hear her across the room. After two weeks, she had tripled her vocabulary, you could hear her across the house and she was walking with her arms down swinging in a proper alternating motion.

There were other aspects of the program including the sensory integration techniques of rubbing various textures over her face, hands and feet. She soon began to tolerate being touched and could play with Play-Dough for the first time without crying. We spun around in circles, had her hanging by her hands from a dowel and started teaching her to read with sight words. The program changed her life but took over mine until I had to call it quits for my sanity's sake.

With all of this stirring, I need to insert a couple of precautions. Too much stirring all at once and your arm can get sore! While the saying is true, "No pain, no gain. No pushing, no progress," we need to keep a realistic pace and balance in our lives.

Getting our kids' needs met is an incredible amount of work. We find ourselves in new roles – advocate, therapist, case manager, medical coordinator. It is easily a full-time job but few of us have the luxury to approach it that way. We need to keep our paying job, decide what to have for supper, plan our next vacation, run a household, kill the crabgrass and take care of the other children.

Compromise will be necessary and sometimes legitimate and important needs will be neglected because we cannot do it all. As parents we are tempted to put the needs of the child with the disability or disease ahead of our own or those of other family members. This can be caused by anxiety or guilt that pushes us to do everything we can for our child. But no one is checking to see if Mom and Dad have been out to dinner lately or whether the three-year-old is getting her bedtime story every night.

We may worry that if we don't do everything or do it just right, we will harm our child or compromise their development. Our guilt and anxiety can cloud our judgment. Instead, we should do what we can reasonably do. Anything we do is helpful and we can still avoid getting burned out in the process.

Our homes are not laboratories, hospitals or schools. Our participation in therapies and services is important, but it must be consistent with our family life. This means that sometimes the exercises have to give way to the bedtime story.

Another caution involves knowing when to keep pushing for solutions and when to accept things as they are. Someone once said, "We've only truly failed when we quit trying." But sometimes our efforts don't bear fruit. We research, seek medical opinions and pray for guidance. But the reality is that there will be times when our efforts to find help fail and acceptance becomes necessary. A helpful prayer at this time is the "Serenity Prayer" which says: "God, grant me the serenity to accept the things I cannot change, the courage to change the things I can, and the wisdom to know the difference."

One of the greatest examples of overcoming setbacks is found in the Old Testament. Nehemiah faced scorn, slander, threats, conflict, fear, discouragement and unbelievable odds as he motivated the Jews to rebuild the walls and gates of Jerusalem. He conquered each obstacle with prayer, followed by action. He did not pray, "Get me out of here," but rather, "Now strengthen my hands."[xxxiv]

Nehemiah showed determination and faith to remain committed to his area of responsibility. He did not focus on the troubles around him, but looked beyond them. He found people who rallied to his cause and worked by his side, brick by brick, until the walls were rebuilt.

We, too, can echo Nehemiah's prayer, by asking God to strengthen our hands as we tackle the responsibility of parenting a child with special needs. We can also seek others to help us in accomplishing our monumental task. That support is invaluable to our success.

In Your Kitchen

1. Ask yourself if you have enough information. Is it up-to-date and accurate?

2. Using the Internet, find one new fact, insight or treatment about the lemon you are facing.

3. List all the traditional and alternative approaches you have tried or are trying. Beside each, on a scale of

one (being no change) to five (dramatic change), rate how that approach has helped your child.

4. Based on the answers to questions 2 and 3, focus your stirring on what is helping the most. Keep a balance with the rest of your life.

9 - PITCHER OF SUPPORT

Lemonade ingredients are stirred inside a container. The lemonade is surrounded, supported and upheld by the walls of the pitcher. If I tried to make lemonade without a pitcher, the lemonade would spread out along the counter and drip onto the floor making a huge mess.

In the same way, we cannot reasonably make lemonade from our sour experiences without being surrounded and upheld by sources of support. The journey of caring for a child with special needs should not be traveled alone. Families, friends and churches often provide support in helping to meet our child's needs and those of the rest of our family. Creating and encouraging a support system is vital to our family's health and sanity. Plus, the best part of the journey is the people we meet along the way.

When we have a problem, it's a special blessing to have a friend we can call and vent our feelings to, someone who knows us well enough to understand how we are feeling and always manages to say the right words. It's a blessing to find solutions to our problems through the willing hands of those around us or through ideas gleaned from the experiences of others. It's a blessing to have someone carry the burden for an hour or more so we can get a break from the incessant demands. It's a blessing to have professionals, as discussed in the last chapter, use their knowledge and training to make a difference in the life of our children.

It is also a blessing to have the real source of hope at our call day and night. We already looked at the role God plays in our journey but I would be wrong to leave Him out of a discussion about support. Others cannot be with me all of the time or in every moment of anguish or frustration, but there is a Friend who promised to never leave me. He is the constant source of help and I can rest in the shadow of His care. He is always alert, always listening and always helpful. I can lean on Him for strength because He has promised to sustain me.

God also provides us with people whom He brings into our lives – friends, family members and professionals. These "angels with skin on" help and encourage us along the journey.

The closest group of support, outside the walls of our home, is often family members. Because they are close to our situation, they know us best, may better understand what we are facing and often know best how to help. On the other hand, because they are close to our situation, they are experiencing the same range of emotions we face and might not be able to support us like we would want or expect. We might wonder why they don't feel the same way we do. Instead, we need to give them room to process their emotions and allow them the freedom to offer support when they are ready.

Jan's extended family members each acted differently. Some chose to ignore Kaylee's problems and diagnosis. Some wanted to say the right things but struggled. Others looked at them differently since they were in the new segment of society that has a child with disabilities.

Lisa's family, on the other hand, has been a tremendous source of support. Lisa's brother was by her side through many of Spencer and Jesse's issues. He is now going to school to become a teacher specializing in autism. Lisa and Rick can go on church retreats or do other things because they know that Lisa's brother can handle the boys while they are gone. Lisa's mother and other two brothers have all been supportive in different ways and it has been a huge help to their family.

My parents and my in-laws have been our babysitters. We don't need to train another person to understand Anna's issues or administer a nebulizer treatment for Joel. The grandparents love our children and have been there every step along the way. There is not stranger anxiety to conquer and our routines and rules are upheld. It works out great for everyone since the kids get to spend time alone with their grandparents and Clint and I can do things without them.

Not everyone has family that is close enough to help or willing to pitch in when needed. We can then turn to our circle of friends. It has been said that in times of crisis, you find out who your true friends are. It has also been said, "A friend is someone who knows the song in your heart and can sing it back to you when you've forgotten the words." I've also heard that "A friend is someone who is there for you when he'd rather be anywhere else." Friends are a gift from God.

Good friends challenge us to be our best. They remind us that we can when we insist we can't. At times, even good friends may fail us, disappoint us or forget to call. But, they also cause us to grow when we would rather not because they care enough to push us. They can encourage us to forgive when necessary and celebrate our victories.

Our existing friendships may flourish or flounder under the pressures of our new situation. Some old friends may have difficulty adjusting to our new circumstances or feel uncomfortable around us. The new demands in our lives may eat up our time and we can no longer invest the energy in maintaining old friendships. Just like when we got married and our single friends drifted away because they could no longer relate, some friendships are for a season of life and will fall by the wayside. Other friends stick for the long haul to journey with us but we need to educate them about the challenges we are facing.

Even if some of our old friends drift away, we have the opportunity to make new friends. In fact, I heard about one woman, upon moving into a new neighborhood, who sent a letter to her neighbors to educate them about her son's condition and to invite them to support her family. Instead of waiting for her neighbors to ask questions and understanding their concern about seeming rude, she opened her heart by writing her family's story. How they learned something was wrong with their child and how it has impacted them. In making the first move, she invited her neighbors to ask their questions. She took a risk, and through her courage to share information with her neighbors, she found friendship in return.

New friends can also be found among other parents of children with disabilities or diseases. We find comfort and validation with others who share our experiences and outlook. It's a relief to not have to explain our feelings and to feel confident that our child is accepted. It also helps to get tips and advice from someone who has been there before us.

When Anna was diagnosed, I contacted the Cornelia de Lange Syndrome Foundation for information. A few days later, I received a phone call from another mother in our area whose son has CdLS. She was my first connection with another parent and, while our children's abilities varied, she offered a listening ear and excellent advice.

My next connection with other families was at a CdLS conference in Dallas, Texas the next summer. It is hard to describe being in a large hotel full of families just like ours. Everywhere I looked, there were children who looked and acted like Anna. In meetings and at meals, I listened to parent after parent offer advice. I listened to others talk about their feelings – and found that I was not alone. It was like a family reunion because we all had a connection through our children.

As a result of a flier handed out at the conference, I joined an online support group. Through a series of email conversations, I cried and laughed with mothers from around the world. I asked my questions, shared my experiences and found solutions to our issues. Through the advice of my Internet friends, many of whom I have never met face-to-face, I was able to diagnose Anna's acid reflux and get medical help for her self-injurious behavior.

For a while after Kaylee was diagnosed, Jan joined a Tuberous Sclerosis support group. She found a group of parents committed to securing funding for research into a cure. Those parents have changed the outlook for children born today but Jan worried that she would become the disease if she didn't find a balance. Today, Jan is part of a support group through her church.

A parents' support group can be described as a safe haven to express feelings that you wouldn't share with your closest family and friends. Members can talk about the grief they are dealing with and their feelings of loneliness. They journey through the stages of denial, anger and resentment. Sharing their pain knits their hearts together. Through time, members can grow from distraught parents having children with disabilities or diseases into strong advocates for their children. Surrounding ourselves with others in similar situations is one way to deal with hardships and learn from one another's experiences. Parents need parents who have walked in their shoes.

Lori remembered her first Autism Society meeting as being an eye-opening experience. "I remember walking in and here was this big circle of women sitting there, all age ranges of children represented, and they were laughing and joking. I thought to myself, 'Their kids have autism. How can they be happy?' I was just thrown by that. I remember one woman talking about her son having a job slicing tomatoes at a sub shop and how proud she was. I thought, "How terrible. How can they be so happy about that?"

It was at this same meeting that someone started talking about a new therapy called applied behavior analysis (ABA). It was a controversial topic since some thought the worst possible thing was teaching your child like you would teach a dog. Others wanted to find out more information and that sparked Lori's interest and pursuit of this therapy for Lucas.

Lori traveled to conferences with some of these other mothers. They would pile 4 or 5 into a hotel room and talk until 2:00 in the morning. "It was the best medicine. That was how I found out about information was from other parents. Whether it was tips on potty training, like sitting them backwards on the toilet, or other things, I found that group of people who knew what worked."

Lori said, "My other friends and family tried to understand but they weren't there in the trenches. They didn't know exactly what I was going through. To me, that was my truly, really saving grace to hook up with parents. We could laugh at things our children did that were really funny but others would think were inappropriate to laugh at. You can't cry all the time. They helped me make it through a lot of things."

When Noah was diagnosed with autism, Shannon and Ray lived across the street from another family with a little girl with autism. The families learned a lot from each other. Shannon also joined support groups focused on speech and later autism. She learned a lot talking to other parents. "It helped us realize this is okay. We are not bad parents. It gave us ideas and ways to help with Noah and different approaches that maybe you wouldn't think of. For instance, we had a time-out box full of squishy balls, play dough and tactile toys for times when Noah was over-stimulated and needed a way to wind down. That idea came from talking to other parents."

Shannon said, "Support groups are vital. But, more vital than organized support groups is being friends with families in similar situations. You can connect and you understand that your child is not just an undisciplined child. If your child pitches a tantrum in public, you don't get the looks or comments. When you have friends that have gone through that, you can laugh and move on."

In addition to offering advice or listening while we process our emotions, friends can pray for us. Roxanne said, "For me, the biggest thing that helped has been the other moms, especially moms with handicapped kids, and their faith – knowing they were praying for us during each stage."

We have the same opportunity to pray for other families we meet along the way. We can pray for those we see in the doctor's waiting room. For the other students in our child's classroom. For the mother facing an autistic meltdown in the middle of a shopping trip. For the parents to have wisdom, strength, and provision.

Thom's original diagnosis came with the warning for the family to celebrate an early Christmas since it would probably be his last. Keith and Linda sent out a call for others to pray and their church, Christian school, family and friends began to pray for Thom's recovery. By Christmas, his stomach was completely back to normal size.

After the chicken pox setback, Thom had several bouts with fluid in his lungs and other byproducts of his disease while waiting to start chemo again. Linda said, "He used these times to rest, meet new friends and to continue to grow spiritually. His uncle, a UPS driver, changed his route so he could stop and visit Thom when he was in the hospital." Keith put out a monthly newsletter filled with Thom's current progress and many were touched by his story and his courage. Linda said, "Everyone prayed his health would continue to improve."

Friends can also do practical things to fill in the gaps of our busy lives. They can take our other children to practices and activities. They can run errands for us. Their extra hands can help with housework. If they see a need, they can meet it with practical actions.

Our local newspaper has a section where people can phone in comments or complaints and they are printed in the editorial section. One item read: "Thank you, flower angel. We don't know whom to thank for planting beautiful flowers around our mailbox. Whoever did it must have known of my husband's bone marrow transplant and our daughter's radiation and found a wonderful way to cheer us."[xxxv] A few simple flowers meant so much to this family during a difficult time.

One husband and wife struggled with their son's serious medical issues; someone had to be with him all of the time. Family members did not feel comfortable taking on his needs but the couple desperately needed time together. One afternoon, the husband opened the door to see his mother-in-law holding a picnic basket and blanket. "I've come to send you and Becky on a picnic this afternoon." She stayed in the house watching their son, while the couple spread out a blanket and picnicked under the large maple tree in their own backyard. They were given time to be alone and time to spend with each other — even though they never left the property lines of their home. Their date in the shade was a gift that Becky's mom could give since she was comfortable watching her grandchild if his parents were just a yell away.[xxxvi]

Several years ago, I read the story of a wife who learned that her husband had been injured in Iraq. She scrambled to find someone to watch her kids so she could fly to Germany to join her husband. Before she could leave for the airport, a friend pulled into the driveway with a care package for the long trip — including magazines, candy, gum, aspirin and a toothbrush. It was the first experience with a network of friends and family who watched over her children, took them to play dates and sports practices and dropped off meals. These friends supported this woman through a difficult time by taking some of her burdens onto themselves.

During some of Thom's chemo treatments, one drug was the worst. They discovered he was able to keep his food down if he got something into his stomach shortly after the chemo treatment. Linda said, "A local restaurant had been a family favorite for years. The owners often played with our children while we ate. They had held Thom when he was only a few months old. So, we made arrangements to get him to that restaurant immediately after the chemo. It began a tradition and everyone loved it. The food could usually be kept down and the old friends were able to renew their friendship."

Another source of support is found within the walls of the home from our spouse and other children. Caring for a child with special needs can be extremely stressful and under such conditions, our interpersonal relationships can suffer. Marriage and parenting are tough enough without the stress of medical bills, fatigue, emotional strain, endless doctor's appointments and social isolation. Adding to these challenges is the fact that couples often deal with their emotions individually. One spouse may be in a completely different stage of the grieving process from the other and communication can suffer.

Marriages under this sort of pressure will either grow stronger or be torn apart. If a relationship was already struggling with communication or financial management issues, the added stress will simply highlight the existing problems. If a relationship is built on a solid foundation, the tools are already there to weather the storm. We need to think of positive, concrete things that we can do to offset the demand and toll this stress can take on our marriages. Marriages can survive and thrive in difficult times if nurtured with time, commitment, faithfulness and love.

It takes effort to find time in the middle of chaos to connect with each other. Perhaps, like the example of the backyard picnic, you will need to recruit the help of friends or family to allow you to get away with your spouse.

The stress can also take a toll on the other children in the home. Like we discussed in Chapter 7, making time to connect with each child helps solidify those relationships. Once again, it may require help from friends and family to make this special time possible.

In return, children in the home can be a source of support for their parents. Lisa's son Joseph is old enough to watch his brothers and sister so Lisa can go run errands, attend a ladies' meeting at church or meet her husband Rick for lunch. He is a tremendous help to her yet she has to balance his help against his teenaged need for independence.

Times together as a family create strong connections able to survive the hard times. Family dinners, movie-nights, game-nights or simply laughing together are times where rest and relaxation can also build relationships. Sherilyn and Adam raced little Matchbox cars and laughed together while waiting for his chemotherapy treatments. When I'm stressed over something Anna has done, a snuggly hug from my little guy, Joel, seems to melt away my tension.

This last source of support may surprise you.

As a mother, I am busy taking care of my children, husband and house. I run the errands, cook the meals, do the laundry, make the appointments, check the homework, administer the medicines, balance the checkbook, clean the house, mediate fights and comfort the hurting. I even have duties outside the home through school events, work and church ministries.

I can provide reassurance to my family by the way I handle crisis. It's like being on an airplane that hits turbulence. If you saw the flight attendants scramble for their seats with white faces and panicked whispers, you would start to panic too. But, if you saw the flight attendants calmly continuing their duties with a smile, their actions would reassure you that everything was okay. We can communicate a similar message to our families.

I read a story about a mother who described how difficult it was for her to maintain her physical appearance when her teenaged daughter was diagnosed with a malignant tumor on her kidney. Previously, this mother had a regular (and extensive) beauty routine and never appeared anywhere without styled hair, full makeup, pressed clothing and jewelry.

One minute they were in the doctor's office and the next thing she knew, she was in the hospital kissing her daughter good-bye as she was wheeled into surgery. The operation took several hours and lasted until after midnight. The weary mother spent the night pacing the floor of the waiting room outside the intensive care unit. It was nearly noon the next day before she was able to see her daughter again.

When her daughter awoke and saw her anxious mother standing there with her clothes wrinkled, her hair uncombed, her mascara smeared and her cheeks colorless, the girl's eyes filled with fear. "Mama, am I going to die?" she asked.

Later, a nurse explained, "Brittany told us, 'I know I'm dying, because my mother would never be seen in public looking like that unless something really, really awful was happening.'" Her mother, who at that moment had lost all interest in wearing makeup and didn't care if her hair was ever combed again, never showed up at the hospital again without looking her best. By presenting a consistent image to her daughter, she helped to reassure the girl that her case wasn't hopeless. She learned what gave her daughter hope and did what was needed to keep that message alive.[xxxvii]

I support my family through what I do. I put the needs of others before my own. But what if I am exhausted, burned-out and stressed? What if I am laid low by an illness or have a breakdown under the stress? How can I continue to give of myself to my family if I have nothing left to give? My life and appearance may begin to reflect my belief that my needs belong last on the priority list.

Truth is revealed in the instructions given by flight attendants on an airplane. They tell us that in the event of an emergency, oxygen masks will fall from the cabinet above and tell us how to put them on. The instructions further state that anyone traveling with small children should attach their own mask first and then their child's mask.

I remember on one flight thinking that my natural response would have been to put the mask on my kids first. Isn't that what I was always doing – taking care of others and not taking care of myself? Weren't their needs more important than mine? In that moment I realized that if my own personal tank was empty, I'd have nothing to give my children and husband. During that flight, God showed me the importance of taking care of my own needs. Not that it's easy to change old habits, but I needed to learn this lesson well for my own sanity.

In the name of loving ourselves, we must avoid operating on overload. When we recognize that we are stressed, tired, overwhelmed, and pressured, take a look at the symptoms. What do they spell? S-T-O-P. The harder it is to stop, the more we need to pay attention, because stopping is the one thing we most need to do. If we ignore the symptoms, we can end up becoming physically ill or clinically depressed. Listen to the warning signals and make a way to slow down.

The first thing to do in taking care of ourselves is to get some sleep. Many of us suffer from chronic sleep-deprivation. We do not always get the sleep that is required. Unexpected circumstances add to our already existing responsibilities so we stay up late to get things done. Or our minds are racing with questions and problems and we have difficulty falling asleep. If we have a child who is ill, we sleep lightly while listening for sounds from their room.

Sleep deprivation can lead to depression, illness and despair. Sleep is critical to our mental and physical health and going without sleep lowers our ability to cope or make good decisions.

If we have enough rest, then everything else will follow. When we are well rested, we are not as anxious. Decisions are easier to make. We feel more energetic and happier. We have the emotional resources to be patient through yet another meltdown by our child.

It may sound impossible but try to sleep when the children sleep. Housework can wait. Our first priority must be rest. To get this vital rest, you may need to get help in the form of another pair of hands around the house. Asking for help is not a luxury, self-indulgence or sign of weakness. It may be a necessity. One form of help comes in the form of respite care. One mother I met resisted the idea of respite care for years. When she finally sent her son to respite care, she went home and slept until after lunch the next day. She hadn't realized how incredibly tired she was or how much of a burden she'd been carrying around. She now regularly sends her son to respite care in order to get a break for herself.

You may also need to make lifestyle changes and reprioritize your activities. After working intensely with Anna for three months with the brain-injury treatment program I previously described, I found myself wiped out. Months of sheer exhaustion followed as I continued to hold my household together by willpower alone. I was later diagnosed with chronic fatigue syndrome and was forced to make sweeping changes to my priorities. Taking care of my health became first priority as I focused on eating right and resting. I cut activities from my schedule, broke down my cleaning chores into manageable chunks for each day and learned to listen to my body to discover when I was pushing too hard. And I made sure that I got enough sleep at night and gave myself permission for naps during the day if I needed them.

Another way to recharge our batteries is laughter. Laughter releases pent-up emotions. It also allows us to see the funny side of our lives. Attempting to cope with the many trials of raising children can be the source of many amusing situations because children do funny things, especially during those times when things don't go according to plan. We can also find laughter by reading the comics, renting a funny movie, watching Bill Cosby reruns or calling someone who always makes us laugh.

Rest, relaxation and recharging our batteries also happens when we change our context and get out of the house to be with different people or try a different activity. As we free our minds from the persistent situation, change gives us a second wind and we can come back with new energy. This is the same principle behind vacations. Choose something that engages your full attention, and has nothing to do with your problem. It could be anything from taking painting lessons to going to lunch with friends.

I could visit a friend or walk to the corner store. I could go sit in the park and watch the people go by. If you can't get out of the house for even a brief period of time, you could turn your bathroom into an inexpensive mini-spa while someone else watches your children. Activities such as exercise, reading and crafts are also good stress relievers.

I shouldn't feel guilty about taking some time to be by myself and regroup. I like to do scrapbooking and to feel like I'm getting something done. I enjoy reading because it's nice to escape to another world from time to time. After I get refreshed, I can then focus on the needs of my child and family.

So, how does a mother find time to take care of herself when her children's needs are so demanding and unending? First, get out a pencil and paper. Name your most immediate needs and be honest. I need more sleep. I need time to take a shower, wash my hair, or get a haircut. I need some new clothes. I need help with the housework, laundry and shopping. I need exercise. I need time to myself. I need someone to talk to who understands. Write down what you need.

Then, share your needs with others and make a plan to get your most important needs met. Plan to get at least one of your needs met on a daily basis, even if it is just five minutes on the phone with a friend. Surround yourself with people who encourage you and help you.

Last, make another list of everything that you do right. Tell yourself that you are doing the best you can.

In addition to finding time to get our personal needs met, rest and recharge, what can we do to encourage a circle of support?

First, we need to be willing to ask for help. Let go of struggling alone. Let go of having to do it all by yourself. It takes courage to let others know of our needs and ask for help. God did not intend for us to walk this journey alone but if we don't communicate our needs and express our concerns to friends, our needs may go unmet.

Never underestimate how the faith and love of our friends can impact our lives. Mark tells the story of a paralytic man and his four friends. These four saw the needs of their friend and conquered many obstacles including a roof in order to bring their friend to Jesus. Seeing the faith of the friends, Jesus healed the man.[xxxviii]

Second, we must be willing to accept the help of others, even if we didn't ask for it. Sometimes God's answer to our prayers comes in human form, but our grief, anxiety, sense of isolation or pride prevents us from hearing and receiving their message of help. We must learn to listen and allow others to give. If not, we may be rejecting the very answer to our prayers.

Third, we must find a balance when communicating. On the one hand, it is important to be honest about our feelings, frustrations and needs. We are not required to be noble, suffering martyrs. It's okay to vent our feelings and talk about how we really feel. Sometimes when talking it out, we start to hear ourselves and get a little insight into the situation. Sometimes we just let off steam and relieve the pressure of our frustration.

On the other hand, we may tend to focus on the positive things when we talk about our child because we don't want to be perceived as a complainer. Certain details about our lives may never come up in conversation. Others may not see how hard we are working and think we are smoothly handling everything that comes our way. We are like the duck who seems to float serenely on the water while paddling like crazy underneath.

Many of us work hard with and for our child while putting on a cheerful face for the world. We know we need people's concern but don't want their pity. However, the image we portray may also shut out empathy and help. Others may think that we're handling things well when the reality is very different. We need to find the balance and give our listener a realistic picture of what our lives are like without dumping our load of complaints in their unsuspecting laps.

Last, show appreciation for all who help and support you. Write a thank-you note to a doctor or therapist. When venting with a friend over lunch, pick up the tab. Give your spouse and children a hug and thank them for helping carry the burden.

In addition to sharing our needs with others and accepting help, here is some advice, gleaned from many parents and sources, that you can pass along to your support system. These are lessons about how to be a friend to a caregiver. You can even add some ideas of your own when you ask specifically for help.

The first category of advice is what to say (or not to say) to parents and caregivers.

It's okay to say, "This stinks" or to acknowledge a person's pain. Our words should be sweet, loving and kind. Words such as "I'm so sorry this has happened" or "What can I do to help?" soothe those who are hurting.

It's nice to hear people ask things like "Is he growing? Is he sleeping through the night?" But don't say "I know how you feel" unless you really do. Sometimes I think, "How could you possibly know how I feel? You haven't had a child with a disability."

Try not to make philosophical judgments like "God doesn't give you more than you can handle" or "Everything works together for good." They are too hard for a caregiver to hear when in the middle of a crisis. If you don't know what to say, simply offer a hug and a silent prayer.

Don't ask questions that make them recount the whole ordeal. Just pick up from where you were the last time you were together and let the conversation flow.

Don't offer advice unless you are asked for it. Sherilyn had many people approach her and tell her what vitamins and treatments Adam should be taking. She even had one woman call her and tell her it was Steve's fault that his son had cancer. She was reading some book and, if you go to page such and such, it says right there that when a father and son are at odds with each other and don't have a close relationship, it releases such and such things and this is the source of leukemia. Sherilyn said, "You don't need people to fix your problems or tell you how to fix them and you don't need people to tell you what you are doing wrong."

Don't approach the family in tears. It makes them feel as if they have to use their energy to encourage you. If you can't stop crying, come back later when you can be tear-free or write a note.

Phone calls are great, but don't expect a call back. Just leave a message that says, "I just want you to know that I'm thinking of you." A short e-mail works too.

The second category of advice is what to do. First, ask the family what they need or what you can do to help. The need may be as simple as washing baby bottles but that may be all it takes to ease the load.

Other things you can do:

- Organize people to help with cleaning, laundry, yard work or shopping.
- Invite them out to dinner or offer to bring over a meal. Understand that some caregivers just can't leave the side of their loved one.
- Offer to take older children to their activities.
- Call when you are going shopping and find out if there is anything you can pick up for the family.
- Make sure you and others are not sick when visiting or coming to help.
- Arrange a movie night or game night for the adults to have fun with other adults.
- Offer to baby-sit or take the children to your house for a sleepover so the couple can spend time together. Or create a romantic evening for a housebound couple.
- Be available for emergencies and give them your cell phone number.
- Be a friend. Listen, care and pray. Offer your

hands and a willing heart.

If a child is hospitalized, don't bring stuffed animals or other large gifts. They are just things that need to be moved from room to room and take up space in a crowded hospital room. Food is a useful gift because it can be shared with the nursing staff. Food is also handy when the parents discover they haven't eaten anything for the past 12 hours.

The last category of advice covers when others meet and interact with our children with disabilities. You may be there to help the parents but don't ignore the child because your failure to acknowledge them feels like a rejection. Make eye contact, say hello, and smile. Be yourself and show friendly interest. Be considerate and patient because it may take them a little longer to get things said or done. Give them your whole, unhurried attention. Understand that they have many unique interests and ask about them. Treat them how you would wish to be treated were the roles reversed.

All of the lemonade ingredients have been stirred together in the pitcher. Are we done yet? No. It's time to sit and chill for a while.

In Your Kitchen

1. List your sources of support.

2. Make a list of your current needs that are being unmet.

3. If you need help, ask one person for something specific this week. Is there someone you can ask for help that you haven't yet?

4. Thank one member of your support system with a note, phone call, e-mail or hug.

10 - CHILLING LEMONADE

"Just chill, would you?" "Chill out." "Take a chill pill."

Have you heard these statements before? In their slang way, they are instructions for us to sit back and relax. Instead of continuing to push forward, we are urged to take a break and wait for the rest of our group or project to catch up.

In the context of making lemonade, after stirring the ingredients together, the next step is to chill the lemonade mixture or put it on ice. Just when we think that we're done, we get to wait.

But what are we waiting for?

We wait for the next round of tests to see if there has been a change in our child's condition. We then wait for the test results. We wait to see if surgery or other treatments will be necessary. We wait for medication changes and we wait for phone calls back from the doctor's office.

Jan waits to see if Kaylee develops any additional symptoms like throwing up or headaches as a result of her brain tumor. She is in a difficult waiting game since she doesn't want to see her daughter suffer or start running into walls as she loses her coordination. Yet, the tumor is in a location where doctors can't (or won't attempt to) operate because of the potential side effects of the surgery. Their neurologist has told Jan to "Save your strength because you have difficult decisions to make down the road." So while they wait to see what develops, Jan shows Kaylee the world and celebrates each day with her daughter.

Sherilyn, Steve and Adam wait to see if Adam's blood counts remain clear of leukemia. They also wait to see if there are any long-term side effects from the extensive chemotherapy. While continuing to be monitored, Adam lives a normal life.

For my nephew with Legg-Calve-Perthes disease, they waited for his hipbone to die, for it to dissolve, for the bone to re-grow, for the next x-ray to see if it was growing in the right spot and now wait to see if his leg will continue to grow at the same pace as his unaffected leg. In the meantime, he wasn't allowed to run or jump for three years during the process. He waited to play tag with his friends at school.

We wait for our child to achieve developmental milestones. We wait for the first smile, first time they roll over, first words and first steps. We wait for successful potty training. Shannon and Ray waited five years for Noah to talk.

We wait for the first tooth to come in and later for the first tooth to be lost and replaced with a permanent one. With Anna, we spent almost a year after having her very loose front teeth pulled until we saw the first corner of their replacements come down. It was another six months before she lost her next tooth.

Since there usually aren't instant results with the various treatments, therapies and programs we try with our children, we wait for the process to work. We wait for growth and change to take place even when we cannot see them or measure daily progress.

We wait for meetings with educational teams and to develop individualized education plans. We put our children on waiting lists for Medicaid waivers, family support and adult services.

We wait to see what the future holds.

What happens while we are waiting? A lot, but most of it happens beneath the surface. Our inability to see what it happening, however, doesn't mean that God isn't working behind the scenes. I learned this simple yet profound lesson from a crocus bulb.

Two weeks after Christmas, when Anna was in the first grade, I received a priceless gift. It wasn't the little clay pot filled with green shoots and a single purple blossom that captured my heart. No, the true gift was the lesson it taught me about being a parent of a child with special needs.

As a new mother, I had big dreams for my children as they grew up. However, despite my best intentions, reality presented a different story in our house. When Anna was diagnosed with CdLS, we embarked on a different journey and her challenges stretched our family.

Not only do children with special needs have the same list of skills to master as typical kids, they need more repetition and time in order to learn them, special equipment, extra doctor or therapist appointments, perhaps a special diet, special exercises assigned by the line of therapists and teachers, a communication method or device to master and an extra emphasis on consistency and routine. As a parent, it didn't feel like there were enough hours in the day. And there were days it didn't happen like I had planned. I would agonize over not having done enough to help Anna develop to her fullest potential, forgetting that God was in control.

To the parent or teacher who struggles with guilt over their inconsistency, I dedicate this story of a very special Christmas present I almost didn't get. When Anna was in the first grade, her self-contained special education class planted some crocus bulbs in September. The crocus bulbs were going to be Christmas presents for the children's families. They would bloom in the middle of winter and remind everyone that spring was coming. So the children planted the bulbs, watered them and put them in the refrigerator. (This was to fool the crocus bulbs into thinking that it was a cold, dark winter, even though it was only September.)

Every once in awhile, the children would get the crocus bulbs out of the refrigerator and water them. But the teacher got busy and the children forgot and the bulbs got very dry. When Christmas came, the teacher decided there was a very good chance the bulbs wouldn't bloom, so she decided not to send them home with the children since dead plants aren't very nice presents. So, instead of a plant, I received a peanut butter and birdseed coated pinecone to hang outside in the yard.

The children went home for Christmas vacation and the teacher cleaned out the refrigerator. She watered the bulbs one last time and left them on the counter, wishing that she had helped the children take better care of them. When the teacher went back to the classroom after Christmas, all of the pots of bulbs had new green shoots coming up! Some of them even had flower buds. So the children got to take their Christmas presents home after all – and it was a wonderful surprise! While the flowers were pretty, the lesson of the crocus was the true gift.

So often, as parents, we worry and grieve that we do not always do the best possible things for our children. The truth is, like the crocus bulbs, our children are growing – slowly, quietly, in ways that we don't even see or suspect until they suddenly toss up a new shoot or blossom. And we gasp with wonder and say, "Where did that come from?" Sometimes we've worked for weeks and months – or even years – to get that particular blossom of first steps, zipping a coat, counting to 25 or looking up and smiling when someone says hello. And then one day, out of the blue, the skill we've worked so hard on (and neglected so many days when we were busy with other things) blooms overnight.

God established the harvest principle that whatever is planted will be harvested and He alone knows how long the growing season will be. In the fields, we expect to harvest in the fall after a specific period of time. With people, the timetable gets trickier.

If typical kids have such a wide range of "normal" for attaining developmental milestones, how much time does it take for a special kid's skills to emerge? We can just watch and wait, trusting God to cause growth in secret until the time for the harvest arrives. Only God knows my child – and her growth often comes in a seemingly overnight spurt.

Anna has always surprised us with new skills when we least expect them or have almost given up hope. For example, after cruising around furniture for 13 months, she finally let go and took her first unassisted step at 24 months of age. Later, after two years of working on identifying her letters and letter sounds, she shocked us all by sight reading the first and last names of all of her classmates for Valentine's Day.

Even when things look so dry and neglected that I doubt there will ever be a bloom, the growth I hope for is still there, under the surface, waiting for its God-ordained personal spring. Being a parent is a true act of faith – we just keep on, day after day, doing the best we can and trusting God that our efforts will bear fruit in their own time. We plant seeds, water and weed – then watch and wait patiently while the Father works behind the scenes.

My daughter is steadily growing and I can hardly wait to see what blooms next.

Something else happens while we are waiting. We get the opportunity to grow in our faith, as we trust God to do His work. If faith without works is dead[xxxix], working without faith is useless too. We do our part by stirring and then have faith that God will do the rest according to His will. We have to let go of the results and place them in God's hands.

A gardener can't see the plant a seed will become, but he plants the seed anyway, knowing that the seed has potential and God has great plans. We can only trust Him and His timing as we wait for the harvest.

Sometimes along the way, we may feel we are in the dark, cold atmosphere of a refrigerator and God feels far away or silent. The reality is that God has not abandoned me and He hears my prayers, even if there is silence in return. Someone once said, "With God, even when nothing is happening . . . something is happening." God's silence may mean that He is busy working on my behalf and taking care of what concerns me. He may be asking, "Do you trust Me?" in the silence.

King David also experienced the silence of God. He thought God was slow in responding and told Him so. "How long, O Lord? Will you forget me forever? How long will you hide your face from me? How long must I wrestle with my thoughts and every day have sorrow in my heart?"[xl] David cried out to God to answer but, in the middle of the silence, David also said, "But I trust in your unfailing love; my heart rejoices in your salvation. I will sing to the Lord, for he has been good to me."[xli]

God may appear to be silent in your situation and you may not see His hand at work. It has been said that "The greatest test of a Christian's life is to live with the silence of God." It's amazing to know we can honor God by how we deal with the silent times.

While waiting, we can also take the time to reflect on how far we have come. When caught up in the busyness and business of taking care of our child and family, we sometimes miss the growth that is happening right before our eyes. While chilling, we can step back and evaluate where we were and where we are now. In our journey, it may be impossible to see how far we have left to go – but we can measure how far we have come.

Instead of worrying about Anna's stuttering (and waiting for her to get her thoughts out), I remembered back to another episode of stuttering. The first time coincided with Anna learning to read. It was as though her mouth couldn't keep up with her brain growth. That time, it faded away in a few months. So, the next time around, I saw that she was also making huge growth in her reading comprehension due to a new program at school for her hyperlexia. By reflecting back, I was able to wait patiently for this phase of stuttering to pass. And it did.

Reflecting also helps me praise God for the growth I had forgotten along the way and for the things that were driving me to distraction six months ago that are now gone. I can praise Him again for her first steps and first words. For her vision improving over the years. For the tattling that shows she is now defending herself and her territory. For her reading skills and comprehension. For the resolution of her self-injurious behavior as we treated her acid reflux. For the tactile defensiveness that disappeared so that I can now give her hugs and backrubs. Praising God for the past growth helps me wait for the next answer to prayer.

Soon, it will be time to take the lemonade out of the refrigerator, pour it in a glass and enjoy the cold, tangy sweetness. I can hardly wait to taste the finished product.

In Your Kitchen

1. Make a list of what you are waiting for right now.
2. List at least one thing you have learned while waiting.
3. Reflect back and make a short list of answers to prayer or growth you have seen.

11 - SIPPING LEMONADE

"The biggest surprise along the way is the joy that I have with my boys. I didn't expect to have joy," said Lisa. "I just expected the suffering. But there is joy. There's actually happy joy and then that deep joy even in the midst of suffering. Joy has been the biggest surprise."

You pour yourself a glass of lemonade and take your first sip. The cold liquid fills your mouth and the tart sweetness envelops your tongue. You savor the mixture of sweet and sour before swallowing, leaving a lingering taste behind. You sit back and slowly take another sip. We sip lemonade instead of gulping, making the time to enjoy the moment.

In life's batch of lemonade, there comes a time when we sit back and celebrate the unique combination of who our child is. We enjoy the changes of attitude and faith we find in ourselves. We slow down enough to notice the good times and those moments of pride and joy.

When we start to sip the lemonade, we let go of the dreams we had for our children and open our hearts to who they are and are becoming. Before we were blinded by pain but now we can see the precious gift that God has given to us. Before we felt disappointed to receive a gift we didn't request but now we see the gift we never thought to ask for.

We take a look at the changes in our own lives and find satisfaction. We may lose a corporate job only to find a rewarding career as the mother of a child with special needs. We may lose the sense of security offered by a suburban lifestyle, but find the security only found in a God who is faithful, no matter where our path takes us. For me, I lost the stereotypical perception that special needs are disgraceful and found that God's grace is demonstrated by His commitment to diversity.

We relax and take one day at a time. We don't want to miss the little things along the way. We find time to simply enjoy our children. We have learned about tough love, compassion, patience and doing the best we can under difficult circumstances. We become aware that our child's every achievement and milestone is a moment to be savored and celebrated.

We celebrate what they can do. We celebrate the people who teach them. We celebrate the other kids at school who make our child a part of their lives. We celebrate the people who love them. But, mostly we celebrate our child and the love and joy that surround them. We see their laughter and kindness and are in awe of their determination and perseverance.

We come to the point we can say, "I love you just the way you are."

That's what sipping lemonade is all about – finding something to celebrate. We enjoy the parts of life that are normal, cheering on our child as they compete in Special Olympics or learn how to ride a bicycle. Then, we celebrate the extraordinary when we find it.

Let's sit back and savor the moment with each of these parents. Sip by sip by sip.

Shannon enjoys Noah's smile and his unconditional love toward others. "It's amazing because someone can be mean to him and he will turn around and be their best friend. He doesn't hold grudges. He is a very loving child and he is very aware of feelings. If he sees an animal or person who is hurt or sad, he gets really upset about it."

For their special outings, Noah wants to get ice cream and walk along the railroad tracks. Shannon said, "If you ask him what he wants to do, that's it. He is fun to hang out with one on one. It's all his way and he doesn't have to change for anybody."

Shannon and Ray have also enjoyed Noah's understanding of God. Shannon's brother sent Noah a fireman computer game but their computer had been running really slow and not working properly. When the game arrived, Noah started praying that his game would work. Ray loaded it onto the computer and it worked. The first thing Noah said was, "Thank you, Jesus!" Shannon said, "It's awesome to see that because sometimes you're not sure about his understanding of God."

Their biggest surprise along the way "is speech because we had so many people telling us that he probably wouldn't talk." So, even when Noah talks and talks and talks, they can enjoy the fact he is speaking at all.

A satisfying sip of lemonade.

Jan is focused on celebrating every moment. She takes Kaylee to the movies and to the park. While Kaylee would enjoy a trip to Disney World, she would be just as happy with a poster of Mickey Mouse on her wall.

"What I love about Kaylee is that she is flawless and innocent," said Jan. "She is everything that is pure. I love her simplicity. I think she was the one born with the gift to not realize the horrible, black, evil things of this world. She can be so delightful and wonderful."

Another sip of lemonade.

Thom had always loved sports and his school was competing in a track meet. Thom wanted to participate but, with a huge stomach, Linda and Keith didn't see how it was possible. Linda said, "At the last minute, one of the relay team members could not compete so Thom took his place. The relay meant one lap around the track for each member. Thom took the last leg and, although he came in last of the four teams, his lap was the most exciting. Everyone went along to cheer him on and encourage him. His courage was contagious. We all went around the field with him. He received a medal for his physical effort, but I think he got an extra stone in his crown for the experience."

In his last week of life, Thom went to stay with an adult friend of Linda's for a few hours. She had him help with the garden and then asked what he wanted for lunch. Linda said, "He asked for a ham sandwich but she didn't have any and offered a peanut butter and jelly sandwich instead. Thom told her to borrow some from the neighbor next door. This was quite unusual for Thom to request anything since he went out of his way to go with the flow. The neighbor came to see the boy, sitting in the strawberry patch, who was insisting on a special sandwich. That neighbor later came to the saving knowledge of Jesus through her brief visit with Thom. We had been praying for my friend's husband for some time and he also came to the Lord."

Just two days before his passing, Thom went for a ride on a boat with his maternal grandparents and thoroughly enjoyed his time. Linda said, "Although his pain medication kept him in and out, he loved the ride in the water. He so enjoyed time spent with Grandpa Charlie and this final ride was something special he requested."

At the time, Linda and Keith did not realize that pictures were taken of Thom. A year after Thom's death, Linda felt so lonely, she asked God to let her see that Thom was okay. Linda said, "Although I knew he was well cared for with the Lord, God granted my desire. Pictures were found in the camera at that year anniversary. My parents always printed their film immediately, so I knew God, in His concern for me, had arranged for the pictures to be taken, forgotten and found at the right moment. The picture was hazy but showed Thom waving at the camera with his sweet smile. Oh, that God would care so much for me that He arranged this whole thing was amazing."

Sip.

Rob has many interests and one of them is basketball. He is an avid San Antonio Spurs fan and knows all of the players and their statistics. He played 8 seasons through the recreational league before he got too old to participate in that program. The next year he was on an adult team through a Christian league in Fort Collins. Their team won first place at their tournament and he was very excited about that. "He's the type of kid that owns the win if he only touched the ball when he threw it in from the sidelines. He's not one of those kids that gets depressed if he misses one shot," said Roxanne. "He's excited if he got to play."

Although he had great coaches through the years that were very supportive, Rob would usually only play the minimum amount and often in two or three segments of time. He had been able to shoot several 3-pointers through the years. Roxanne said, "3-pointers are much easier for him because he doesn't have to deal with all that craziness under the basket and figure out who is supposed to do what. He can just be in his own little area. He's never the star player unless you count enthusiasm."

However, there was one game with the adult team where he was needed to play the whole game. It was easier for him to get into the rhythm of the game and he scored a personal record four 3-pointers during the game. Roxanne said, "He was skipping backwards down the court. He told me, 'Just for a minute, I felt like those guys must have felt like when the Spurs got the championship. Just for a minute.'"

Roxanne told others, "I think this will go down in the family record book for a while."

One of the church folks set her straight. "For a while? What are you talking about? This was the night of a lifetime. This will go down in his memory bank for the rest of his life. Let him brag as much as he can because this is a big deal."

Sip.

Right before he turned 16, Rob earned his Eagle Scout rank. In the Boy Scouts program, they have an adapted program available in order to support kids with handicaps but Rob completed the regular requirements. He didn't even choose a small-scale project. He coordinated a wetlands project with over 250 people involved helping him. Roxanne said, "He is very proud of that. He got an Eagle ring and wore it for the first several months. I was afraid that people would make fun of him. I wasn't sure. But it has been amazing the doors it has opened since people will give him a chance once they realize he is an Eagle Scout." Congratulations to Rob on such an amazing achievement!

Sip.

Adam's pancreas shut down and he was hospitalized right before his senior year of high school. He eventually recovered but missed the first three and a half weeks of classes. In addition, he had saved all of the most difficult courses for his last year when he would be past the worst of the chemotherapy treatments. When he managed to go back to school, he was in a wheelchair for the first couple of days as he regained his energy. His teachers didn't give him a free ride but helped him catch up without a lot of the busy work. For the first time in his life, Adam made straight A's taking all of his hardest classes and missing those first weeks. It was a cause for celebration.

Sip.

Lisa likes to take Spencer to nearby Estes Park after she drops her older kids off at camp and then they spend the day in town. "We don't talk. There aren't a lot of words spoken, but he loves to shop. Not just for him but for me too. So, we walk around and shop. One day last summer, we were walking around town and walked into this shirt store. One of them had this really cool logo on it with a dog and the words, 'Life is good.'"

Spencer saw the shirt and said, "Ooo. Life is good." Lisa looked at him and said, "Yeah. You know what? Life is good. Let's buy the shirt." She bought the shirt and Spencer wore it as they went on to buy ice cream and sit by the creek to watch the elk on the other side. Lisa said, "People were walking by walking their dogs and Spencer was talking to the dogs. He wouldn't talk to the people but he would say, 'Hello, Mr. Dog' and the dogs would stop and talk to Spencer. I realized that life really is good. Those overwhelming times come, but life is good."

Spencer loves nature, waterfalls and being outdoors. Jesse, on the other hand, just likes being with Lisa. Jesse is also excited about investigative things and spends most of his day searching for clues and figuring out things. Lisa said, "He's got an engineer's mind so he is trying to figure out how things work. Watching their minds work or seeing brilliant moments is so fun. It's so fun and it really overweighs the hard times. We sit and laugh at some of the things that are said and done between Spencer and Jesse. It's amazing."

The boys love to go to "big movies" in the theater. Lisa said, "Spencer has memorized every movie coming out. He also loves the calendar. He memorizes birthdays and loves celebrations like birthdays and holidays. Christmas is so fun with him, like having a little 3-year-old all the time that is excited about Christmas. I don't ever want that to leave. It's fun to spend Christmas with him because he is so excited. They just enjoy life."

Spencer doesn't have the muscle tone and isn't interested in actually physically participating in a sport. However, he has every interest in doing the sport on a video game and enjoys watching his brother Joseph's football games. Spencer needs to watch for a long time and know everything about it before he will participate. He watches and watches before he tries.

Jesse, on the other hand, is very coordinated and athletic. Lisa said, "He is definitely going to need to be involved in some kind of sports. He now understands a little bit about boundaries and behavior controls, so I think that we could put him on a sports team. He also enjoys being involved in Joseph's sports and being a part of that at sporting events."

Sip.

Lucas worked as a media aide at his high school, shelving books. With his love of organization and structure, it was a perfect fit. Another thing Lucas loves is science and he is doing very well in a regular science class with very little support from his aide.

Lori's biggest surprise was that Lucas has come farther than she thought when she read that first book. "He has really come far from that kid who couldn't talk and sat in the corner and waved his fingers. He is really becoming independent, much more than I thought he would, and that is such a joy. He always likes to help people."

"One of the things I enjoy most is when he watches cartoons like Wile E. Coyote or Tom and Jerry. You know that the coyote is going to get it every time. He laughs from the belly every time like it's the first time he saw it. It's such a joy to have that overwhelming laughter that he has. Most kids would be over that but for him, every time is like the first time. He just can't control that big belly laugh."

When Lucas was in the seventh grade, Lori had to finally tell him that there was no Santa Claus or Tooth Fairy. She said, "Lucas, I have to tell you that Mom is the Tooth Fairy. And he looked at me and said, 'How do you get to all those houses?' I had my 15-seconds of fame because I was THE Tooth Fairy. He is so literal it's sometimes a joy."

Another enjoyable moment happened at their old church when Lucas was going through Confirmation classes. The lesson was on forgiveness and loving your neighbor. The leader said they were supposed to write down the name of somebody they didn't like or they had a problem with. Lucas couldn't think of anyone. Lori asked him, "What about that kid that used to hit you on the bus?" Lucas replied, "No, he's my rival." Lori said, "I made him think of somebody but he said he liked everybody. It makes you think that we are the ones with the handicap. He likes everyone and the few people who have been unkind are 'rivals.' I thought that was a really special thing."

A very special thing happened the first time Lucas said the word "Mommy." He had done the babbling "ma-ma-ma" type of word before but the first time he called Lori "Mommy" was in a complete sentence. He said, "I love you Mommy."

Sip.

In our house, we clapped and celebrated when Anna took her first steps alone. We celebrated when she was able to sight-read her classmates first and last names before she was able to sound out any words. We celebrated when she began to understand what she was reading. We celebrated after her first Special Olympics track meet. We celebrated when she learned to ride a bike and we congratulate her every time she makes progress getting braver in the swimming pool. Anna can now be heard telling herself, "Good job, Anna. Good job."

Enjoyable moments with Anna almost always include her giggles. We play hide-and-seek and tickle her when we find her. Now, she is giggling even before we get close to her hiding place. She always asks for us to do it "again." Singing, dancing, spinning, playing and laughing – she truly lives up to her middle name of Joy.

It has been fun to watch her try new things. I chaperoned an adaptive ski trip and was able to watch her ski with her personal instructor for the day. While on a family vacation, we were invited by friends to go boating on a lake. Anna actually got into the water (with her life jacket on of course) several times. Although she refused to let go of whichever adult was holding on to her, she was willing to get in. She has come far in trying new things and gets braver all the time.

I'm also amazed at Joel and how he is not slowed down by his asthma. He takes great pride in knowing how to turn on the nebulizer machine and hold the mask over his face. If he needs it, he asks for his "breathing medicine" and, afterward, jumps down and runs off. He is full of zest and personality and cracks us up daily with his antics. He is also my snuggle-bug buddy and I'm enjoying every hug and kiss until he outgrows this tendency.

Another satisfying sip.

Sip by sip, we can savor every amazing moment of progress and joy along the journey. The tangy sweetness of lemonade quenches our thirst. Since sipping lemonade is so refreshing, let's share a glass with someone else!

In Your Kitchen

1. Make a list of at least ten moments of joy that you can remember along this journey.

2. This week, pay attention and watch for moments of joy. Stop and take a mental picture of each one. Sip and savor them.

3. Plan how you will celebrate the next achievement and put the plan into action when it happens.

12 - SHARING LEMONADE

"When we knew times of great sorrow," said Linda, "God was there for us. He sends others as His hands and feet. He places special people in the very place He knows we will need assistance. Now, when our time of trial is past, we find we become His hands and feet for the next in line. God is rooting for us and cheering us on. I believe He is proud of our accomplishments. Earth is our testing ground. We grow, change and continue on His path and ultimately will be given a new challenge. Often our experiences can be of use for the next on the path."

It's been a long and difficult process. We have tasted and puckered at the lemons of life. We took the gut-wrenching emotional lemon juice and counterbalanced it with the sweet sugar of hope and faith. Normal life went on and watered down the extremes while our other children added their unique flavor to the mixture. We did our part by stirring with the support of others and waited for God to do His part. In the end, we found joy as we sipped the resulting lemonade.

We transformed the lemons and were transformed by them. Our views of God, our child, ourselves and the rest of mankind have been forever changed. We have lived through and learned the great human paradox – that out of our pain, sorrow and disappointment come growth, strength and love. We may feel proud to have survived the challenge but also find a stronger character and purpose in life.

We may feel we have a great deal to offer others in similar circumstances, so we pull out another glass and share our lemonade with a weary traveler.

Just as we were supported, we support. Just as we were comforted, we comfort. Just as we were encouraged, we encourage. We take what we have learned and pass it on.

We pass it on to others with lemons. Back in chapter one, I said that we shouldn't compare our lemons with those of another because we might feel guilt or envy. When it comes to sharing our lemonade, I again say don't compare your family with someone else's. If their struggles seem worse than our own, it is most likely because we are used to our situation and have found ways to cope with it.

No matter how different other people's lives appear to be, our differences are only in type and intensity. Even if our situations are different on the outside, inside we are dealing with the same emotions because life didn't turn out like we expected it to. In that light, there are many people around you thirsty for a drink of lemonade.

Instead of simply setting up a lemonade stand and waiting for people to come to us, we can share our lemonade through a variety of ways. Here are some opportunities other parents have found.

One mom dreamed of a place where mothers of special kids could gather. Her church stepped in and offered her a room, a coffee pot and childcare for siblings. She made flyers announcing the first meeting of the Special Moms/Special Kids group and the rest is history. The group gives mothers a place to celebrate the impossible. She said, "I have found a lifeline of emotional support. Sometimes just being in the presence of another special mom lets me know I am understood and am not alone in this journey."[xlii] She followed her heart and found other moms who needed her as much as she needed them.

Shannon participates in an "A-team" (autism team) family support group through her local school district. She especially reaches out to the new families whose children are starting kindergarten. She offers them a listening ear as well as advice to help them through the IEPs and what to expect.

I have been an Awareness Coordinator for the CdLS Foundation for several years and even gave a brief presentation at a conference in Chicago in 2004. At conferences and family gatherings, I used to seek out parents with older children to glean their wisdom. Now, I make a point to talk to the new parents and let them know it's okay and they are going to make it through this. Seeing Anna, they are full of questions about how we got to where we are today and I can pass on what worked for us.

Lori went to work for the Autism Society in Wisconsin. Through her work on their newsletter, she was able to recommend resources. She has also led a support group at her church. Now, Lori works as a paraprofessional at an early childhood center and is usually teamed with kids with autism. She is able to talk to the new parents and offer support and advice. "Not that I have answers for them, but I'm trying to pass on what I have learned from other parents," said Lori.

Roxanne has used her experiences to gain credibility as a speech pathologist. She has always tried to help parents with their chronic grieving and can now speak from the heart. She has led parent support groups and language preschools through the years, working closely with parents. "It's really helped my credibility when I can say, I have a child who has a rare form of Down syndrome and this is how we dealt with it. Yes, we have a younger child who is smarter and we have to deal with that too. It's made me more real when I talk to parents."

Roxanne's outlet is not just professional but through her involvement in women's ministries at her church as well. "I've been amazed at how many people God has brought into our path after we lost Sunny that had also lost children. We've used that experience over and over to share with people and encourage them. So many women are dealing with issues with their kids, whether they're actually handicapped or just getting through whatever the latest stage of behavior is. I've been able to be open and transparent about our challenges and share with them."

Lisa shared what she has learned by speaking at MOPS and at a women's conference out of state. She said, "There are so many people who are still stuck in that place of despair. We live in a society where we are all supposed to be perfect and, when your child isn't perfect, you are fighting to try to make it even look like he is. I want to encourage people that this might be a different walk than your neighbor, but it's okay."

Lisa not only sees a need for encouraging books for parents raising autistic children, but also books for those children to be able to understand about hope and living in Christ. With her understanding of how her boys think, she wants to develop a series of children's books on the fruit of the Spirit that the autistic mind can comprehend.

Jan is also looking ahead for opportunities to share what she has learned with a larger audience through speaking and writing. After sitting with Kaylee through numerous medical tests, she saw a need for books at a child's level to explain what MRIs or CAT scans do. "It's a scary experience for the kids but most doctors don't know how to explain it at their level," Jan said. "I'm working on several books to put in hospitals and clinics to help children understand and not be afraid."

Others look to share lemonade through the context of their church. One church in our area has a Special Friends ministry that offers a support group for parents, a separate Vacation Bible School program for kids with special needs and respite nights for families. Jan participates in that Special Friends group and Lori helps with the respite night for families in our community.

Feeling accepted and being able to participate in social settings is important for everyone, including our kids with special needs. This sometimes isn't possible due to unfounded fears, a lack of education about specific needs and the simple unwillingness of others to get involved. Great strides have already been made in educational and recreational settings and now many churches are starting to see this need and act on it.

Our church had a program in conjunction with the elementary aged kids church that paired special needs kids with a teenaged volunteer who was always within an arm's length away. They are now in the process of launching a Helping Hands, Helping Hearts ministry to send trained adult volunteers into other Sunday school and activity settings so kids with special needs can participate.

Some churches have designed Sunday school classes for children with special needs while others have a class for adults. These classes have adapted materials for the developmental level or physical skill of the participants. In one such class, a mother colored the Bible story pictures in advance, leaving a few things out so the student could add items to the picture during class and feel like they helped create the craft.

Sharing lemonade doesn't have to take place on a grand scale or in a public arena. You can also share lemonade with a single individual through a note, a phone call, a visit or an offer of help. By offering a listening ear and a quiet prayer, we can encourage another cook who is busy in their kitchen of life.

Please notice that at this stage we are sharing lemonade, not lemons. When we were in the middle of juicing our lemons and struggling with the variety of emotions, it was helpful to share those feelings with someone else in order to work through them. When we talked about the support of friends and family, there were those we could be brutally honest with about our reality and what we needed. Not everyone can handle the raw emotions or complaints and we need to choose wisely whom we share our lemons with and how often we unload our pain.

In this context, we need to pass along encouragement and advice to those with their own struggles. Parents facing a load of lemons don't need to hear or carry our complaints and frustrations too. Instead, they need a listening ear, understanding, hope, encouragement and practical advice to help them through another day. Offer refreshing lemonade instead of sour lemons. They have enough of those already.

Hearing a practical solution to our current issue gives us hope that we can get beyond this point. Often, the helpful advice we received at a low point is what we in turn pass along. Here is a sampling of the best advice and encouragement some parents have received and what they would say to parents with a new load of lemons.

One mother said, "I'm no martyr. I am simply Kiley's mom under very straining circumstances. My message to you is that you're not alone in your journey, your feelings are very real and your task of parenting is extraordinarily difficult. We speak the same language and my heart goes out to you."[xliii]

Avoid the what-ifs. They are deadly. They can crush your spirit and smother your hope because they carry your thoughts and imagination to places you will never visit. Most of the time, what I worry about never happens. Instead, realize that today is the tomorrow you worried about yesterday.

Another mother said, "I know the shock of discovering that your child is blind, but trust me, your tears will dry. You won't cry when you someday see what your daughter can do."[xliv]

"Remember that children with learning disabilities are not dumb. They just learn differently."[xlv]

Lori said the best advice she received was from someone who told her "to keep my chin up and keep at it. You just have to pull yourself up and go. In those first few months, I wondered how I was going to do that. But, it was true."

Lori's advice is to find and get early, early intervention because it makes such a big difference. She also said to find a circle of friends and hook up with other families. Then, "Find joy. We decided years ago, that no matter what the challenge was, this is the only life Lucas is going to have and so I try, not always successfully, to concentrate on what he can do and not what he can't do. I've learned, with my friends, to be the one laughing instead of the one crying. There are always sorrows but you have to find happiness."

Roxanne said the best advice she received was to "always see them as a child first and not as a kid with such-and-such diagnosis. Look at him as a person and a child first and not as his handicapping condition."

The best advice Lisa received came from her son Spencer on the day she had a breakdown. "It's going to be okay. The sun is going to rise tomorrow and there is hope." As society is learning more about autism, Lisa said now is a turning point for families to be accepted and not have to pretend their children are perfect. "All I have to do is say autism and people know why he is throwing a fit at Wal-Mart or why I'm overwhelmed to the point that I can't even talk right now. All I have to do is say one word and they understand. That's a huge hope for us as parents."

Someone told Jan, "Fear and faith can't walk hand in hand." She was trying to live with both fear and faith instead of making a choice and commitment to trust God with the future. She said, "The bar is always being raised but I look at it now as an opportunity to rise to a new plateau. The bar is being raised higher but that makes it closer to God." Jan's advice is to find out through the school district what your child is entitled to and what help is available for you.

Somewhere along the line I heard the saying "Where there is life, there is hope." My advice is to find out everything you can, do everything you can and leave the outcome in God's capable hands. I realized that Anna is not defective even if there is a mutation on one of her genes. She is just carrying extra burdens and, because she is, so am I.

The best advice Shannon received was from the doctor at PROMPT who said, "Stop teaching him sign language and he will talk." As Shannon said, "It was contrary to what every other professional was saying but it worked. Because sign language was easy for Noah, he didn't try to talk."

Shannon's advice is to relax. "You've got to remember that they can't help the way they are behaving. It's not the end of the world. Sometimes we get so uptight because we think about what everybody else thinks and we need to just focus on our child and not worry about everybody else. Just relax and know that God is going to take care of it."

She also added, "Make sure you do your research because there is a lot out there and a lot of good advice. And pray, pray, pray. Lord, give me strength for this next five minutes!"

With the help of God and others, we have transformed our lemons into lemonade but we have also been transformed and changed by them. Our messes have been turned into messages of hope for others. In addition to advice and encouragement, we can pass along the lessons we have learned through our time in the kitchen.

Sometimes we are asked if we would change our lives. For Anna's and Joel's sakes, I would wish life could be easier for them, but, when I think of how I have grown, I wouldn't change a thing. Because walking by faith through the difficult places of life is where I've experienced God's faithfulness like never before. Those are the places where my perceptions, values, and priorities have been shaped. Where I've learned that the little irritations of life are just that – little irritations – and nothing to derail my day over.

Linda said, "The most important thing we learned was that things like clothes, houses and cars are replaceable. The important things are the people in our lives."

Linda had several dreams about going into a restaurant and

requesting a table for four. She began to feel God was letting her know that although Thom was doing well and hope was high, the end result was they would be a family of four. About the same time, she found a book about Mary and Joseph. Linda said, "Just as Mary and Joseph were chosen to be Jesus' support system, so Keith and I were chosen to help Thom through the rough times of his trial. Although it was a terrible time for us as a family, in fact the trial was for Thom. That made quite a difference in my attitude. I began to look on the daily difficulties as a step. Thom grew spiritually during this time and began to share his story with others. His outlook was so positive and upbeat that all were amazed."

Thom went to be with his Heavenly Father at the age of nine. Linda said, "He was ready to go to his Father so we were able to let him go. But it was the toughest situation we ever had to deal with and I am sure we did more growing through this ordeal than at any other time. It seems we grow through trials and tough times but when things are going well, we often stagnate and lose ground."

One parent learned that God is not cruel but is infinite in love and goodness. "Of all the things that I would not have chosen, having a handicapped child ranks at the top. Of all the blessings in my life, Liana has been the greatest and she has taught me that 'the greatest of these is love.' The most important thing I've learned from Liana is that we're all handicapped and that God loves us just as we are. He does not need to heal us and make us perfect in order to love us. If we were all perfect, we would not need Him and we would not need each other."[xlvi]

Another parent has discovered "the gift of my newfound compassion for children with hidden disabilities, my desire to help them and the joy I feel in using all my hard-earned knowledge to guide another parent through the complex maze of his or her own journey."[xlvii]

A weekend sermon came as a timely reminder to me. The speaker told the story of a parent who asked God to make their handicapped child whole. In reply, God said, "No. His spirit is whole, but his body is only temporary." The speaker went on to share that the spirit goes deeper than the cortex. Our bodies are a home that holds our spirits. Regardless of whatever part of the home may not be working properly, there is still a spirit residing there that can love and be loved.

While Anna's understanding and comprehension may be limited, deep down she has a spirit that is reaching for a relationship with God. I have to trust that the Bible stories we read together and the worship songs she listens to and sings are reaching further than I can see.

I am learning that I can't set limitations on my children. I want them to reach their full potential. CdLS is part of who Anna is, but it certainly doesn't define her as a person. When I look at her, I can see her the way God must see her – through eyes that reflect unconditional love and acceptance.

In seeing our child's potential, we sometimes see the potential in ourselves as well. How many parents and siblings have gone on to study social work, physical therapy, speech therapy, special education, or enter the medical field? Simply because they were inspired by a loved one? Who better to stand beside someone in a crisis and know how they are feeling? Who better to pass along comfort and support?

I was an overachieving perfectionist before Anna was diagnosed with CdLS. I have come to love, accept and value the imperfect in life. After all, that's how God loves, accepts and values me. While I was still in sin, He reached out in love to save me. I'm also learning to relax in areas and focus on the things that matter most.

Lisa has learned to live in reality. "This is real and I can't sit and think that things are going to be perfect. I need to understand that life is not supposed to be without suffering. That suffering produces perseverance, which produces character, which gives us hope because Christ loves us. It was a big, big step for me to come to accept the reality that I had a special needs child."

Lori and her husband Scott used to live in southern California before they had children. She said, "It was fun and possessions were important. But, they're not anymore." She also said while she would want life to be easier for Lucas, "He is who he is and he has made us who we are. I wouldn't change it."

Lori said, "I've grown the most in my acceptance of (or adjustment to) the fact that I now know it's okay. We're just here for a short time. I wish I had not hung on to so much instead of turning it over to God. I am a worrier by nature but, when you let some of it go and turn it over to God, it's amazing. I wish I would have done that sooner." Lori also "learned to listen to that little, small voice inside of me."

Shannon learned to "trust God through everything, because no matter what, He will give us the strength for whatever we're dealing with." When asked if she would change anything, she said, "I would want no surgeries, no therapy, no being left out for Noah but we have all learned and grown along the way. My oldest is so compassionate towards a person with special needs or anybody who is a little different. He is the one to talk to them at school or stand up for that child. If he didn't have these experiences with Noah, I don't know how he would react. We have all gained empathy for others."

So, let's pull out another glass, pour some lemonade and share it with another.

In Your Kitchen

1. Write in two or three sentences how your perspective, values and priorities have changed as you made lemonade. How has your mess been turned into a message?

2. Make a list of three main pieces of advice you would give to someone in a similar situation. These might include what you wish someone had told you at the beginning of your journey.

3. This week, identify someone else facing a lemon

situation that you can encourage. Take the time to reach out through a phone call, email, letter or visit. Share with them something you have learned along the way.

13 - FOLLOWING A RECIPE

Juice the lemons. Add sugar and water. Stir, chill and serve.

As far as recipes go, lemonade is an easy one. It's also not an exact science. Many times the recipe will say, "Adjust to taste." Experienced cooks adapt and change recipes all the time, so why should the recipe for lemonade be any different?

You can adapt the recipe for your family. Every family is different and every batch of lemonade is unique. It's an experiment in the kitchen of life as you create your own variation with the guidance of God.

Am I done making lemonade? Not by a long shot! Anna and Joel keep giving me opportunities to transform (and be transformed by) the lemons of life.

In fact, just today, Anna had a major meltdown over breakfast. She first wanted oatmeal, then toast and then back to oatmeal. I made the oatmeal and she cried that she didn't want it. So – I made her eat it while listening to her whine. The next act came as all three siblings fought over the computer and who would get to play their game first. Crying, hitting, wrestling and tattling meant another lemon for Mom.

Am I done making lemonade? No, because life is full of lemons.

In fact, every family, with or without disabilities, has

challenges. Some disappear, others remain – and they are all different. Plus, not all of our lemons as parents have to do with our children. Many lemons we encounter are just a part of life.

You may face lemons at work through a job change, a conflict with a co-worker, a demanding boss or an impending layoff.

You may face financial lemons of debt, unexpected bills, the sale of a house falling through or identity theft.

You may face the loss of a relationship through a death, a move, a divorce or other conflict.

You may face disease personally, in your spouse or in other family members.

Guess what? No matter what kind of lemon life brings, juicing that lemon creates emotions of anger, denial, guilt, blame or depression. Life still goes on and we can process these other lemons using the same strategies contained within the pages of this book.

So, as you look at your pile of lemons, roll up your sleeves and get to work. There's a batch of refreshing lemonade just waiting to be made.

In the meantime, hang on to these promises. Jesus said, "In this world, you will have trouble. But take heart! I have overcome the world."[xlviii]

Paul wrote, "So we're not giving up. How could we? Even though on the outside it often looks like things are falling apart on us, on the inside, where God is making new life, not a day goes by without His unfolding grace. These hard times are small potatoes compared to the coming good times, the lavish celebration prepared for us. There's far more here than meets the eye. The things we see now are here today, gone tomorrow. But the things we can't see now will last forever."[xlix]

So, take your new lemons, follow the recipe and make more lemonade.

In Your Kitchen

1. Pick another lemon in life to process next.

EPILOGUE

Within the pages of this book, you have met some amazing families busy making lemonade and learned about their children. They have shared their emotional journey, strategies and advice with you. Do you wonder where they are now? As of January 1, 2011, here is an update.

Anna, age 14, is in the 8th grade. She continues to grow academically in the intensive learning program, especially in her reading. She is very healthy and is entering puberty. She recently had four teeth pulled to make room for her permanent ones to come in and may need future orthodontic help. She is on a Special Olympics basketball team and is looking forward to track in the spring. She receives speech therapy, occupational therapy and adaptive physical education at school. Anna also is never far from her plastic balls decorated with Elmo and Dora the Explorer. When she grows up, she wants to be a writer – a fact her mom, Candee, is very proud of.

Joel, age 7, is now in 1st grade and becoming a good reader. His asthma and allergies are under control with medications and he has been able to have sleepovers at his grandparents without any negative side effects. He loves to play with Legos and has decided he wants to be in the Coast Guard when he grows up. His mom, Candee, is very proud of his recent decision to accept

Jesus into his heart.

Lucas, age 19, participated in his high school class graduation in 2009 and is now attending Community Connections, a school district program for ages 18 to 21. Over the past several years, his family tried many dietary changes but, in the end, none changed anything. His mom, Lori, said she is especially proud of his developing independence skills including riding the bus and doing his laundry.

Joshua, age 17, is a junior in high school. During the school year, he is back on track with his organizational and focusing skills. Last summer, he received tutoring at the reading clinic and made great improvement in his attention. His mom, Lori, is especially proud that he is a caring young man with a usually positive attitude.

Thom would have turned 42 last summer. During his 14-month battle, he led many to the Lord. A few days before his death, he told his parents that he would check out heaven for them so when it was their turn to come, he could show them all the good spots.

David, age 35, works at Wal-Mart in the produce department as he has for the past five years. He was approved for a house through Habitat for Humanity and moved into his new home in December of 2008. His mom, Sherilyn, says this move gave David his own home and his life, as he now talks a lot at work in addition to taking on the challenges of mowing the lawn and paying his bills the day they arrive. He still takes medicine for a chemical imbalance.

Adam, age 24, finished two years at a junior college, is playing hockey and has a job selling high end televisions and speakers. He is still free of cancer and continues to be periodically monitored. However, as a side effect from the chemotherapy, he and his wife of four years are finding it difficult to conceive. His mom, Sherilyn, is especially proud of his attitude and his witness for cancer improvements and for Christ.

Kaylee, age 14, is a freshman in high school. In February 2007, an MRI showed that the giant cell astrocytoma in her brain was growing but later tests show it has stabilized. Despite increased behavior issues and mood disorders, Kaylee shows progress with her social interactions and conversations. She suffers chronic functional pain which medication has been unable to resolve. Her mom, Jan, is especially proud of Kaylee's sense of humor and acts of kindness.

Noah, age 14, is in the 8th grade and being mainstreamed 80% of the day with 20% of his time receiving special education services. He now wears hearing aides. He still swims every week and looks forward to another season with Special Olympics. Teenage hormones began to show themselves through temper issues, self-injury and trying to run away. His parents started him on a medication which seems to be working well. His mom, Shannon, is especially proud of Noah's big heart and his love for Jesus. She says Noah is always thinking of other people's feelings.

Spencer, age 14, is in the 8th grade. He is independent and loves his school. His parents tried an anxiety medication which altered his behavior dramatically. Once weaned off the drug, he returned to his normal behavior. His mom, Lisa, is especially proud of his visual contact, caring for family friends, and his longing to be part of a family community.

Jesse, age 10, is in the 4th grade. He is fully integrated in the regular classroom with a paraprofessional aide but gets support from the autism class as well. He works at grade level with excellent classroom behavior. He loves to stay in contact with his friends. While he continues to have rollercoaster emotions, the upsets are fewer and further apart and he can now be reasoned with. His mom, Lisa, is especially proud of the way he cares for his older brother, Spencer, and his desire to be in a close family unit.

Rob, age 20, graduated from high school with a regular diploma and was accepted into college. He is currently working toward a certificate in CAD drafting and welding. After years with a mild hearing loss, Rob now has normal hearing because his ear canals grew during puberty. His mom, Roxanne, is especially proud of Rob's work ethic, perseverance, and gracious spirit.

APPENDIX
LEMONADE RECIPES

Basic Lemonade

Ingredients
- 4 cups water
- 1 cup lemon juice (or 4 to 5 fresh lemons, juiced)
- 2/3 cup sugar

Directions
1.   In a pitcher, combine the ingredients and stir until the sugar dissolves. Serve immediately over ice or chill until serving time.

Lemonade

Ingredients
- 1 ¾ cups white sugar
- 8 cups water
- 1 ½ cups lemon juice

Directions
1.   In a small saucepan, combine sugar and 1 cup water. Bring to boil and stir to dissolve sugar. Allow to cool to room temperature, then cover and refrigerate until chilled.
2.   Remove seeds from lemon juice, but leave pulp. In pitcher, stir together chilled syrup, lemon juice and remaining 7 cups water.

Old Fashioned Lemonade

Ingredients
- 6 lemons
- 1 cup white sugar
- 6 cups cold water

Directions
1.   Juice the lemons to make 1 cup of juice. To make your labor easier, FIRMLY roll the lemons between your hand and the counter top before cutting in half and juicing.
2.   In a gallon pitcher combine 1 cup lemon juice, 1 cup sugar, and 6 cups cold water. Stir. Adjust water to taste. Chill and serve over ice.

Vintage Lemonade

Ingredients
- 5 lemons
- 1 ¼ cups white sugar
- 1 ¼ quarts water

Directions
1.   Peel the rinds from the 5 lemons and cut them into ½ inch slices. Set the lemons aside.
2.   Place the rinds in a bowl and sprinkle the sugar

over them. Let this stand for about one hour, so that the sugar begins to soak up the oils from the lemons.

3.   Bring water to a boil in a covered saucepan and then pour the hot water over the sugared lemon rinds. Allow this mixture to cool for 20 minutes and then remove the rinds

4.   Squeeze the lemons into another bowl. Pour the juice through a strainer into the sugar mixture. Stir well, pour into pitcher and pop it in the fridge. Serve over ice.

Pink Lemonade

Ingredients
- 2 cups white sugar
- 9 cups water
- 2 cups fresh lemon juice
- 1 cup cranberry juice, chilled

Directions
1.   In large pitcher combine sugar, water, lemon juice and cranberry juice. Stir to dissolve sugar. Serve over ice.

Never Bitter Lemonade

Ingredients
- 6 cups water
- 1 cup white sugar
- 1/8 teaspoon salt
- 12 cup fresh lemon juice

Directions
1.   In a pot combine water, sugar and salt. Bring to a boil and continue to boil for 2 minutes. Chill the sugar water for at least 60 minutes in the refrigerator.

2.   In a 2-quart pitcher, mix cooled sugar water and lemon juice together. Pour over ice and serve.

Passionate Pink Honey Lemonade

Ingredients
- 1 cup water
- 3 fresh strawberries, sliced
- 1 cup white sugar
- ½ cup brown sugar
- 1 teaspoon honey
- 7 cups water
- 1 ¾ cups fresh lemon juice
- 2 slices orange

Directions
1.   In a saucepan, combine 1 cup water, strawberries, white sugar, brown sugar and honey. Bring to a boil, and simmer 10 minutes, stirring occasionally. Cool to room temperature, cover and chill.
2.   In a large pitcher, mix together water, lemon juice, and orange slices. Stir in cooled syrup; chill. Serve in a tall glass over ice.

Blackberry Lemonade

Ingredients
- 4 cups water
- 1 cup sugar
- 1 cup lemon juice
- 1 tablespoon grated lemon peel
- 1 cup blackberries
- 2 drops of blue food coloring (optional)

Directions
1.   In a large saucepan, bring 2 cups of the water and all of the sugar to a boil.
2.   Boil for 2 minutes, stirring occasionally. Remove

from heat; stir in the lemon juice, lemon peel, and remaining water. Cool slightly.

    3. In a blender, combine 1 cup of the lemon mixture and the blackberries; cover and process until blended. Strain and discard seeds.

4.   Pour blackberry mixture and remaining lemon mixture into pitcher. Stir well. Add food coloring if desired. Refrigerate until chilled.

Cherry Lemonade

Ingredients
- 1 cup hot water
- ¾ cup sugar
- 4 cups cold water
- ½ cup fresh lemon juice
- 6 ounces maraschino cherries, undrained

Directions

1.   In a large pitcher, combine hot water and sugar; stir until sugar is dissolved. Add cold water, lemon juice and cherries with their juice.

2.   Mix well. Serve over ice.

Citrus Lemonade

Ingredients
- 4 lemons
- 4 limes
- 4 oranges
- 3 quarts cold water
- 2 cups sugar to taste

Directions

1.   Squeeze the juice from the lemons, limes and oranges. Pour into a gallon container. Add water and

sugar. Mix well.

2.   Serve on ice with additional fruit slices if desired. Store in refrigerator.

Fresh Strawberry Lemonade

Ingredients
- 1 ½ cup freshly squeezed lemon juice
- 6 cups of water
- 10 ounces frozen strawberries, pureed (fresh would do perfectly well)
- Sugar to taste

Directions

1.   Combine lemon juice, water, and ¾ of the strawberry puree. Add sugar until you have reached the desired tartness/sweetness. Add strawberry puree until the strawberry/lemon taste balance is about equal.

Watermelon Lemonade

Ingredients
- 8 cups seeded watermelon cut into 1-inch chunks
- 1 cup hulled and quartered fresh strawberries
- 1 cup granulated sugar
- ½ cup freshly squeeze lemon juice
- 2 cups water (approximately)
- Thin watermelon wedges with the rind (optional)

Directions

1.   In a food processor fitted with a steel blade, pulse the watermelon, strawberries, and sugar until blended and smooth. Strain through a fine-mesh strainer into a 2-quart container, pushing down on the solids to get all the juice.

2.   Add the lemon juice and enough of the water to

make 1 ½ quarts. Chill until very cold.

3.   Serve over ice with a wedge of watermelon, if desired.

Raspberry Lemonade

Ingredients
- ¾ cup sugar
- ½ cup water
- 1 cup fresh lemon juice (about 4 lemons)
- 3 ½ cups water
- 1 container (10 ounces) frozen raspberries in syrup, thawed
- ¾ cup water

Directions

1.   Mix sugar and ½ cup water in 1-quart saucepan. Cook over medium heat, stirring once, until sugar is dissolved. Cool to room temperature.

2.   Mix cooled sugar syrup, the lemon juice and 3-½ cups water in 2-quart nonmetal pitcher. Place raspberries in strainer over small bowl to drain (do not press berries through strainer). Reserve berries for making ice cubes. Stir raspberry liquid into lemon mixture; refrigerate.

3.   Spoon raspberries evenly into 12 sections of ice-cube tray. Divide ¾ cup water evenly among sections with raspberries. Freeze about 2 hours or until firm. Serve lemonade over ice cubes.

ABOUT THE AUTHOR

Candee Fick is the wife of a high school football coach and the mother of three children including a daughter with Cornelia de Lange syndrome and a son with allergy-induced asthma. In addition to her personal experiences in the realm of special education, she was a volunteer Awareness Coordinator for the CdLS Foundation.

She has published a dozen articles in publications including *Exceptional Parent* and *Special Education Today*. Her first book, *Pigskin Parables: Reflections of a Football Widow*, explored what football and faith have in common. She also writes Christian romance and is a content editor for a small Christian press.

When not busy with her day job, writing, or speaking, Candee can be found shuttling her kids to various activities or reading a good book. She and her family make their home in Colorado.

For more information, to contact the author, or sign up for her email list, please visit www.CandeeFick.com.

MORE BOOKS BY CANDEE FICK

<u>Standalone Fiction</u>

Catch of a Lifetime

<u>The Wardrobe Series</u>

Dance Over Me
Focus On Love
Sing a New Song
A Picture Perfect Christmas
Home For Christmas

<u>Within the Castle Gates</u>

Stepping Into the Light
To Win Her Heart
The Lost Heir
Finding Home
Saving Grace

<u>Non-Fiction</u>

The Author Toolbox: Practical Tools to Build a Book, a
Platform, a Business, and a Career
Pigskin Parables: Exploring Faith and Football
Pigskin Parables: Devotions from the Game of Football
Devotions from the Garden
Be Like a Tree
Creation Declares

BIBLIOGRAPHY

Carroll, Bruce. <u>Sometimes Miracles Hide: Stirring Letters from Those Who Discovered God's Blessings in a Special Child</u>. West Monroe, Louisiana: Howard Publishing, 1999.

Gill, Barbara. <u>Changed by a Child: Companion Notes for Parents of a Child With a Disability</u>. New York: Doubleday, 1997.

Mullins, Traci, General Editor. <u>Irrepressible Hope: Devotions to Anchor Your Soul and Buoy Your Spirit</u>. Nashville, TN: W Publishing Group, 2003.

Osborn, Susan Titus and Janet Lynn Mitchell. <u>A Special Kind of Love: For Those Who Love Children with Special Needs</u>. Nashville, Tennessee: Broadman & Holman Publishers, 2004.

Stallings, Gene and Sally Cook. <u>Another Season: A Coach's Story of Raising an Exceptional Son</u>. Little, Brown and Company, 1997

Thomas, Bernadette and Cindy Dowling, Editors. <u>A Different Kind of Perfect: Writings by Parents on Raising a Child with Special Needs</u>. Boston: Trumpeter, 2004.

END NOTES

[i] Learning Disabilities Association of America website statistics at www.ldaamerica.org

[ii] Asthma and Allergy Foundation of America website statistics at www.aafa.org

[iii] Statistics from the National Institute of Mental Health found at www.pediatrichealthchannel.com/adhd-children/index.shtml

[iv] Autism Society of America website statistics as of February 2007 at www.autism-society.org

[v] Cystic Fibrosis Foundation website statistics at www.cff.org

[vi] National Association for Down syndrome website statistics at www.nads.org

[vii] United Cerebral Palsy website statistics at www.ucp.org

[viii] National Osteonecrosis Foundation at Johns Hopkins website statistics at www.nonf.org

[ix] Spina Bifida Association website statistics at www.sbaa.org

[x] Tuberous Sclerosis Alliance website statistics at www.tsalliance.org

[xi] Cornelia de Lange Syndrome Foundation website statistics at www.cdlsusa.org

[xii] Statistics from article at www.emedicine.com/ped/topic2587.htm

[xiii] Genesis 1:31 and Psalm 139:13.

[xiv] Stallings, *Another Season*, 17.

[xv] Tuberous sclerosis information at www.ninds.nih.gov/disorders/tuberous_sclerosis/tuberous_sclerosis.htm

[xvi] Statistics found at http://en.wikipedia.org/wiki/Down_syndrome

[xvii] Gill, *Changed by a Child*, 11-12.

[xviii] John 16:30.

[xix] Stallings, *Another Season*, 22.

[xx] Ibid., 24.

[xxi] 2 Corinthians 4:8-9

[xxii] Gill, *Changed by a Child*, 54.

[xxiii] Mullins, *Irrepressible Hope*, 233.

[xxiv] Isaiah 55:9.

[xxv] Matthew 19:26.

[xxvi] Matthew 1:23b.

[xxvii] Lamentations 3:23.

[xxviii] Carroll, *Sometimes Miracles Hide*, 52-53.

[xxix] Osborn, *A Special Kind of Love*, 171-172.

[xxx] Stallings, *Another Season*, 163.

[xxxi] James 2:17

[xxxii] James 2:18

[xxxiii] Thomas, *A Different Kind of Perfect*, 102.

[xxxiv] Neh. 6:9

[xxxv] Loveland Daily Reporter-Herald, R-H Line section, 6/12/07

[xxxvi] Osborn, *A Special Kind of Love*, 113.

[xxxvii] Mullins, *Irrepressible Hope*, 167-169.

[xxxviii] Mark 2:1-12

[xxxix] James 2:26

[xl] Psalm 13:1-2

[xli] Psalm 13:5-6

[xlii] Osborn, *A Special Kind of Love*, 102-103.

[xliii] Thomas, *A Different Kind of Perfect*, 70.

[xliv] Osborn, *A Special Kind of Love*, 127.

[xlv] Ibid., 45.

[xlvi] Carroll, *Sometimes Miracles Hide*, 99.

[xlvii] Thomas, *A Different Kind of Perfect*, 56.

[xlviii] John 16:33b

[xlix] 2 Cor. 4:16-18 The Message

www.ingramcontent.com/pod-product-compliance
Lightning Source LLC
Chambersburg PA
CBHW031511040426
42445CB00009B/180